THE
WAR
WITH
MEXICO

BY THE SAME AUTHOR

HISTORY

Goodbye to Gunpowder
The Birth of the Constitution
July 4, 1776
Valley Forge
The Battle of New Orleans
Victory at Yorktown
The Great Separation
The Tide Turns
The Siege of Boston
The War in the North
The Great Conspiracy

BIOGRAPHY

Elizabeth I
  A Great Life in Brief
John the Great
  The Times and Life of John L. Sullivan
The Gentleman from New York
  A Biography of Roscoe Conkling
Sir Humphrey Gilbert
  Elizabeth's Racketeer
Sir Walter Raleigh
  That Damned Upstart
Marlborough
  The Portrait of a Conqueror
Bonnie Prince Charlie
  A Biography of the Young Pretender

THE WAR WITH MEXICO

Donald Barr Chidsey

WILDSIDE PRESS

© 1968, by Donald Barr Chidsey

All pictures courtesy New York Public Library Picture Collection

To the
Whiteheads,
Barbara
and
Bill

Contents

1	Palm Sunday in the Morning	9
2	Fulminations of a Dictator	15
3	"Thermopylae Had Its Messenger—"	22
4	The Great Remembering	31
5	Hiss the Villain	39
6	The Cut-Ups	47
7	Blood out of a Dream	54
8	The First Dark Horse	62
9	The Hot Potato	68
10	Dark Doings	75
11	Jacta Est Alea	81
12	Two Romps	87
13	A Tough Nut to Crack	95
14	Voyage to Hell	100
15	A Delicate Situation	106
16	'Twas a Famous Victory	112
17	Army and Navy Together	119
18	The Big Blast	125
19	In the Footsteps of Cortez	131
20	A Jar of Marmalade	140
21	The Dream City	145
22	Sober Men and True	151
23	A Good Day's Fighting	157
24	Fury Among the Generals	166
	Notes	170
	A Note on the Sources	180
	Bibliography	181
	Index	189

CHAPTER

1

Palm Sunday in the Morning

THE AIR WAS CLAMMY and streaked with fog when they marched out of Goliad, meaning to go to Victoria, the morning of March 19, 1836. Visibility was poor, so that it was almost ten o'clock by the time they had all got across the river.

There were about 350 of them, and they had nine small fieldpieces and a howitzer, together with sundry supply and ammunition wagons pulled by oxen. They were not Texans, these men. The colonel, James W. Fannin, a Georgian by birth, had lived in Texas for two years, but the others were freshly arrived in the war area from Tennessee, Georgia, Alabama, Louisiana. They were young men, quick to grin. Most of them carried muskets, though a few might have had rifles. A rifle would shoot farther and more accurately, but it took longer to reload, and for this reason soldiers going into battle preferred the old reliable musket.

They had all heard that the Mexican Congress had decreed that anybody caught entering Texas with an unauthorized weapon in his hands should be treated as a pirate— that is, killed on the spot. They had *heard* this, yes; but it was hard to believe. Not even a greaser would behave like that. The cause was a just one—the cause of independence, of defiance of oppression—the same cause their grandfathers had fought for half a century earlier; and the Texans, the real ones, the residents, were men like themselves, their kind of folks. Besides, things at home had been slow. So here they were, joshing and singing, these young volunteers.

True, it was known as a fact that the great Santa Anna was proceeding north with giant strides, and that a wing of his army, under his right-hand man, General Urrea, recently had arrived at Matamoros in the southeastern corner of the province, or republic, and might be expected to move in this direction. But it all seemed very far away, and unreal; and besides, everybody knew that the greasers were slow.

Fannin's boys were traveling over prairie, though there were belts of timberland, and ahead of them was Coleto Creek, the banks of which were well wooded. That stream was about ten miles from the town of Goliad; and about two miles short of it, in a depression that had been burned over and where the grass was growing in again, the colonel ordered a halt to give the stock a chance to graze. Some of the officers protested that the spot was exposed and urged him to push on to the creek and the shelter of the trees, but he snorted, having little use for Mexicans. If the officers had insisted, if they had taken it to the men, the story might have been different. Volunteers, as distinguished from regulars, in the old American tradition elected their own officers, and by the same token they could depose them any time they disagreed with them. But the men, in this case, did not seem to care.

They had rested about an hour and a half, and the order to hitch the wagons again had just been given, when a large force of Mexican cavalry appeared out of the trees on the right. They moved very fast, getting between the volunteers and the creek, and they were followed by a big body of infantry, also moving fast. There must have been more than a thousand men in all.

They wasted no time. They got into position, and then charged, cavalry first, followed by infantrymen with fixed bayonets. Fannin was cool, as indeed were the boys, though this was their first fight. They formed themselves into a loose square, three lines deep, the wagons in the center, the fieldpieces at the corners, and calmly started to empty saddles.

The Mexicans fell back. General Urrea rallied the cavalry and in person led it toward the volunteers again, but it was no use; the horses could not take it, and neither could the men.

Then there was another infantry charge, the officers with drawn swords behind the men. Once again, it was no use. They stumbled back in confusion.

Fannin's men were not faring too well either. Something had gone wrong, as so often happens in an army, and the provision wagons were missing. Also, there was no water. The fieldpieces could no longer be fired, for they had clogged and could not be swabbed out. The wounded lay everywhere, groaning. The surgeons, Bernard and Shackleford, had to treat them by feel, for there were snipers all around the camp and nobody would risk a light. It was chilly, it was damp, and the men were hungry, tired, thirsty. Yet there were only three desertions that night: Mexican sentries killed all three.

Earlier, Fannin had called the men into conference, pointing out that right after the falling of full darkness they could probably make it to Coleto Creek in a dash. Some would be lost, to be sure, and they would certainly have to leave the wounded behind. What did they think? There were about sixty wounded, at least forty of them so badly that they could not be counted upon even to crawl. Fannin himself had been shot in the upper leg, but he went on hobbling around.

The men voted against the dash. They would stick it out, and see if they could get terms the next day.

It was a long, terrible night.

In the morning Urrea was reinforced, and now he had field guns with grape shot, which he proceeded to use. During the night the volunteers had thrown up earthworks, but these were no good against grape.

It was proposed to surrender. Fannin himself was against this. "We beat 'em off yesterday, and we can do it again today," he said. He was overruled, and submitted. A white flag was raised. There was a parley between the lines. Afterward the men were told—and there is not the slightest doubt that the parleying officers believed this—that they would be treated as prisoners of war and would be sent back by ship to New Orleans, presumably after they had given their parole not to play any further part in the Texas Revolution. On this assurance they laid down their arms.

The officers' sidearms were put into a separate chest, and the officers were told that these would be given back when transportation had been arranged.

Heavily guarded, they were marched back to Goliad, where they were locked in the church, which was not large enough for them. They were uncomfortable, but as soldiers, even volunteers, they were accustomed to this. They were fed very little, and they did not have the means to make fires, but they remained in good spirits. They sang "Home, Sweet Home," and told one another about their parents and their sisters.

They were there a week. On the fifth day eighty-two volunteers from Nashville, Tennessee, were somehow jammed in among them. These lads had been seized down by the coast when they disembarked. They, too, thought that they would be released as soon as arrangements could be made.

Saturday night, March 26, there came to Lieutenant Colonel Portilla, the commander officer at Goliad—Urrea was temporarily absent—a message from Santa Anna himself, a man who was not only the commander-in-chief of the Mexican army but also President of Mexico, and who was now at San Antonio. Santa Anna pointed out that invaders with weapons in their hands were to be treated as pirates, by order of Congress; and he should know, for he had handpicked that particular Congress himself. Here it was a week after the fight, and word had come to the generalissimo that the prisoners were still alive. Let them be executed immediately.

Portilla, a decent man, was distressed, as were many of the other officers, but they knew better than to protest an order from the President. A few volunteers who could be proved to have been empty-handed were spared, as were the two surgeons, who would be needed to take care of the many Mexican wounded, and a few of the officers some Mexican women took pity on and hid. The rest were awakened at dawn, and told to get ready to march. They thought that they were going home at last.

It was Palm Sunday.

They were separated into three columns, one starting in the direction of San Antonio, another that of San Patricio, the third that of Copano on the coast. They were in double file, and infantry marched on either side, with cavalrymen, lancers, closing up in the rear.

"*Pobrecitos!*" the Mexican women murmured, as they watched the boys being escorted out of town; but the boys did not understand that, knowing no Spanish, so they went on singing.

About a mile from town—far enough away so that the wounded in the hospital would not hear anything—all three columns were halted. The soldiers turned to face them, and cocked their muskets, and stepped back.

"My God!" somebody screamed. "*They're going to shoot us!*"

Some fell flat, some dropped to their knees to implore

mercy, a few ran away to be killed by the lancers,[1] but most of them, frozen in astonishment, simply stood there and were slaughtered. It took several volleys. Afterward the soldiers went in with their bayonets, lunging at everything that twitched. They piled the bodies and covered them with brush and oil and set fire to them. Almost undoubtedly some of the men were still alive at that time.

Fannin and his lieutenant colonel, Ward, another Georgian, were paid a gruesome honor when they were shot apart from the rank and file. Fannin was quiet about it. He handed his watch to the officer in charge, asking that it be sent home to his wife. He also asked that he not be shot in the head and that his body be given a decent burial. They shot him in the head and tossed his body in with the others.

Ward was not so polite. When they ordered him to kneel he told them to go to hell, and he was still shaking his fists at them and cursing them when they mowed him down.

There were still the wounded, back in town. They were hauled out of their beds, or shot or bayoneted right there, and their bodies were piled in a courtyard and set afire. They did not burn well. All the next day the *sopilotes*, the buzzards, were working on them.

That's the kind of war it was.

CHAPTER

2

Fulminations of a Dictator

ANTONIO LOPEZ DE SANTA ANNA *was* Mexico in its early days as a republic. He knew his fellow countrymen and, except for a little while in the beginning, they knew him, and did not trust him, but called him in to head the government only at times when his talents were urgently needed, as too often they were. An officer, technically a gentleman, he was no scholar—his many proclamations, more bombastic even than was usual at the time, were written for him; but he was a professional soldier, having joined the Spanish colonial army at the age of fifteen. He had seen a great deal of rough guerrilla fighting, the putting-down of bandits and petty revolts, and he was not queasy about spilling blood. He liked to be called "the Napoleon of the West," but in truth he was not much of a general, and won his battles only when the forces under him enormously outnumbered those of the enemy.[2]

He was languid sometimes, but capable of spurts of terrific energy. He could move fast, though which *way* he might move next was something that nobody knew. He was a good administrator, but he did not care for the routine of the presidency and always preferred to rule through a dummy, while he himself supervised the aggrandizement of

ANTONIO LOPEZ DE SANTA ANNA

his estates near his hometown of Jalapa, in the province of Vera Cruz. For he was very rich; though how he got that way it was better not to ask. It was in the main house of these estates that Fanny Calderón, the Scottish-born American wife of the first Spanish ambassador to the Republic of Mexico, was to meet him (and Fanny was no fool):

"In a little while entered the General Santa Anna himself, a gentlemanly, good-looking, quietly-dressed, rather melancholy-looking person . . . apparently a good deal of an invalid, and to us decidedly the best looking and most interesting figure in the group. He had a sallow complexion, fine dark eyes, soft and penetrating, and an interesting expression of face. Knowing nothing of his past history, one would have said a philosopher, living in dignified retirement —one who had tried the world and found that all was vanity, one who had suffered ingratitude and who, if he were ever persuaded to emerge from his retreat, would only do so, Cincinnatus-like, to benefit his country."[3]

Mexico had won its independence in 1821, and the next year adopted a constitution that called for a great deal of states' rights, with a fairly weak central government. Santa Anna jumped the right way at this critical time, and was rewarded by the first President, Iturbide, who made him a brigadier and the governor of Vera Cruz province—at twenty-seven.

Iturbide went on to make himself an emperor, but not for long. A group of generals, among them Santa Anna, threw him out. As a result, Santa Anna might have cut himself a big slice of the patronage pie; but he preferred to stay in Vera Cruz, where he was the complete boss, and to keep accumulating estates around Jalapa, all the while watching for his big chance.

It came in 1829, when the Spaniards mounted a ludicrous attempt to reinvade and reconquer Mexico. This attack, absurdly feeble, always doomed to fail, came from the east, Spain's side, and Santa Anna, as governor and military commander of Vera Cruz, was the Man on the Spot. He didn't do much—he did not need to—but what he did do he did with a flourish, and when the pitiful "invasion army," cut off from its supplies, denied naval support, at last surrendered with all honors of war, Santa Anna, who accepted that surrender in person, made the most of it. He was now a popular hero, who could do no wrong—for a while, anyway. The Mexicans are an emotional people.

Bustamante, the current President—they came and went —was a friend; but when Bustamante's foot slipped, Santa Anna the hero was there to grab power. He still shied away from the presidency, striving for a little while to rule by means of a series of dummies. He learned that he could not count upon deputies to draw all power to Mexico City, so at last he consented to assume the presidency himself, whereupon he hamstrung the Congress and declared that the constitution of 1824, to which he had sworn everlasting allegiance, was null and void. In other words, he made himself a dictator.

The expunging of a national constitution is not likely to go unprotested. There were squawks from several of the states, and the loudest squawk came from Texas.

It was a vast sprawl of land bounded by the Sabine River to the east, the Gulf of Mexico to the south, the Rio Grande to the southwest. It extended north and west nobody knew how far, though it did not include California, a separate province in the Mexican governmental scheme of things. There were those in the States who contended that Texas had been included in the Louisiana Purchase, a notably hazy deed, but this opinion was never held in Mexico, and anyway the government at Washington had specifically disavowed this claim when it purchased the Floridas from Spain in 1819.

Texas presented a problem. It should be rich land, but it was so far away, so hard to get to, and there were few roads or even trails traversing it. The young Republic of Mexico tried to interest possible settlers, offering all sorts of inducements, and tried too, a little later, to settle the place with convict labor. Nothing worked. On the other hand, there was this gringo Moses Austin in Mexico City just pleading to be permitted to lead parties of his fellow gringos into Texas for permanent settlement. The government at last agreed, with certain stringent restrictions, and Austin, a Connecticut Yankee, became the first of the *empresarios*, or immigration contractors.

There was nothing in the terms that would prohibit the settlers from bringing their own guns, for it was assumed that they would need these for protection against the various Indian tribes of Texas, a fierce lot, not at all like the submissive Indians of most of the rest of Mexico. It was surely *not* assumed, however, that the settlers would form themselves into para-military bodies, a sort of homespun militia, when things did not go the way they liked.

The newcomers were required to take an oath of allegiance to the infant republic, which they did readily enough, and they were also required to profess the Roman Catholic faith, which they did not do. Roman Catholicism was a state religion in Mexico, where the Church was very strong, very rich, and like the Army an institution always to be taken into consideration, no matter how laic the matter at issue. The Church in Mexico, unlike the government, was not much interested in faraway Texas. It sent an occasional priest, who prowled from place to place, christening and marrying, rites that under Mexican law could only be performed by such as him. Often enough, since the priest might visit a given village only about once in two years, the marriage and the christening were both in the same family. There were no masses, there was no communion. No church buildings were put up.

When the republic was formed, Texas did not have a large enough population to rate as a separate state, and so it had been coupled with the large neighboring state of Coahuila. This made it mighty inconvenient for the Texans, especially after the capital was moved from the Rio Grande to Saltillo, many miles in the interior, several days' painful journey for the Texans, who complained that they were underrepresented anyway. Why, asked the Texans, couldn't they be made into a separate state, now that they had the required population? Hadn't as much been implicitly promised?

Slavery was another prickly question. It never had existed in Mexico, where there were virtually no Negroes, and where the Indians, meek creatures, made ideal laborers, peons. The republic did not even take the trouble to prohibit slavery, at first. The Texas settlers, however, for the most part came from southern states—when they formed their first council at least forty-two of the fifty-eight councillors were natives of slave states, six came from the middle or New England states, four were British, and the other six were of unrecorded origin—and they had always taken slavery for granted. Some of them brought their slaves with them, and presumably others would do so. Their contention was that cotton was obviously the best crop for a land like Texas, and a cotton crop without the help of Negro slaves was unthinkable. Mexico City, D.F., did not like this glib explanation, and in 1829 the government formally banned slavery. The following year it banned immigration. Neither ban made much difference to the testy Texans, who ignored them.

Lately, however, there had been mutterings in Mexico City, and there was talk to the effect that these high-handed Yanquis must be taught respect for the law of the land.

This matter alone could have caused trouble, but when the new President, Santa Anna, airily dissolved Congress and pronounced the 1824 constitution extinct, an act that at the same time ended the pitiful little Coahuila-Texas legislature, Texans reached for their guns.

They made it clear that they were doing this only in defense of the constitution. Like the colonists along the east coast of America a little earlier, they insisted that they were only claiming what they were entitled to; and as the British colonists clamored for a return of their rights as freeborn Britons, so the Texans, at first, demanded that they be treated as real Mexicans.[4]

This was too much for Antonio Lopez de Santa Anna. He scraped together an army of about 6,000, intended to reinforce the army his brother-in-law already commanded in Texas. The treasury was empty, as usual, but he managed to raise $400,000 from private lenders who charged only 4 percent interest—a month.

Santa Anna shared or pretended to share the growing Mexican conviction that all of these recalcitrant immigrants in Texas were incited, in the first place, by the American government, which planned eventually to take over the whole territory. It was all a plot, he swore. And if the Yanquis tried to do anything to stop him when he stamped out the revolt, he told the British ambassador, he would tear right through them and plant the Mexican tricolor in the middle of Washington.

He started north.

CHAPTER

3

"Thermopylae Had Its Messenger—"

IT DID NOT SEEM POSSIBLE, when the church bells rang the morning of February 23, 1836, in San Antonio de Béxar,[5] that it was not a false alarm. Men told themselves that Santa Anna simply *couldn't* have moved all those Mexicans that fast.

A little peering out across the plain proved, however, that Santa Anna had. This was no outflung scouting party. It was the van of an army, five or six hundred dragoons about eight miles away on this side, the San Antonio side, of the Alazan River.

There were no horses left in San Antonio, which is the reason why no scouts had been sent out. It had rained a lot recently, and there was no dust to mark the horsemen, nor was there any sunlight to fleer off their buttons and weapons, so that they had seemed to appear suddenly, like a phantom force. But they were real enough. And they were coming toward the town.

Lieutenant Colonel William Barret Travis ordered a retreat to the Alamo. He had about 150 men, all volunteers, a few of them Texans. He shared the command with Colonel James Bowie, a celebrated frontier fighter, always a tough man to contend with, though just now he was coughing his life away in the hospital at the Alamo—galloping pneumonia.

The Alamo was not a fort. It never had been. It was a monastery built by the Franciscans in 1718 and long since desecularized. The church, the oldest building, had stone walls four feet thick, but the roof had fallen in, and there were no firing slits. The church was a short distance away from the space enclosed by walls, a rectangular space 154 yards north and south, 54 yards east and west. There were no towers, redoubts, coigns, slits, bastions, not even a firing step. The walls, made of dirt, were 2¾ feet thick and from 9 to 12 feet high, but they had been put up only for the purpose of protecting the surrounding settlers and their livestock from marauding redskins. The tock of an arrow they could take, but they would be like paper before cannons.

There was a moat or fosse outside, but it was not much of a deterrent; there was no water in it, and it did not go all the way around.

In short, this was anything but a stronghold. It had been used in the past as a military post, a barracks, and parade ground for various small Spanish army outposts,[6] but now it was more or less in ruins.

It was hard to leave the town. They had taken it two months earlier, after the dirtiest kind of house-to-house fighting, and they had released its defenders under Perfecto de Cos, who was inspector general of the Mexican Army, a lucrative post, and the brother-in-law of President Santa Anna himself, after accepting Cos's word that he would stay south of the Rio Grande for the rest of the war. Now they had to give it up. As a town, it was indefensible.

A small rear guard was left in the plaza, with orders to retreat to the Alamo as soon as the enemy entered the town. This force was commanded by a middle-aged man in buckskin, a man who had recently appeared from Tennessee, having walked most of the way, together with a dozen others he had picked up as he went along, all asking to be shown where the action was. This man was a "character." He had served three terms in the House of Representatives in Washington, and he could tell a merry story. He called his Kentucky rifle "Betsy" and was reputed to be a crack shot. He also carried a fiddle, and could wham out a tune anytime anybody felt like dancing. His name was Davy Crockett.

The town of San Antonio de Béxar was not in itself much of a place. It commanded no mountain pass; the countryside for many miles around was pancake-flat. It did not control a navigable stream; the San Antonio River at that point in that season was a mere creek. Neither was it situated upon a crossroads, and it was very far from the American border from which help might be expected. Why, then, was it to be defended? Only a fool would try to hold such a place. But Travis and Bowie *were* fools—fighting fools.

They had orders from both Henry Smith, provisional governor of Texas, and Sam Houston, who had just been elected commander-in-chief of the Texas army, to quit the town at the approach of Santa Anna's men, first doing what damage they could to the Alamo, and to haul away as many guns as they were able, dumping the rest into the river.

Bowie and Travis chose to disobey, to make their own decision. They were utterly serious about it. They believed that unless Santa Anna was checked there, at least for a little while, there would be no stopping him. San Antonio was almost 150 miles from the nearest part of the Rio Grande, but Travis and Bowie regarded it as the gateway to Texas, and they were determined to hold it, as they said in firm letters to their superiors. What's more, the men under them agreed.

They knew how weak they were, and they sent for reinforcements. They did not have anywhere near enough men to post the walls, even if those walls had been proof against artillery. Their own guns were not very heavy—four- and six-pounders, thirty-odd of them, taken from General Cos, but most of these could not be mounted, and anyway there was not enough powder.

One bit of luck they did enjoy. On the very day when the Mexican advance guard was sighted, only a few hours after that event, the men who had been digging a well inside of the Alamo grounds gave a great shout. They had struck water.

This was important. The river was several hundred yards away, and though there were irrigation ditches from it along the east-and-west walls, these could easily be choked off by the besiegers, who would not even have to expose themselves in the process. But now they had their own water.

By late afternoon the dragoons were poking into the southern part of town, and Crockett and his men quietly retired to the Alamo.

An officer rode up, carrying a white flag, but he never raised a parley. They banged a cannonball right near his feet, spraying him with dirt; and he got the idea and rode away. After that, a red flag was run up in the Mexican camp. It meant: No quarter. In addition, and lest there should be any doubt about it, the buglers over there sounded the *deguello*, which meant the same thing.

As for the defenders, they had a flag too—the red-white-and-green flag of the Republic of Mexico. For as far as they knew, they were still citizens of that country.[7]

Colonel Travis made mention of that flag the next day when he wrote to the provisional council at Washington-on-the-Brazos, a note in fact addressed to all the world:

Commandancy of the Alamo
Bejar, Feby. 24th, 1836
To the People of Texas & all Americans in the world:

FELLOW CITIZENS & COMPATRIOTS—I am besieged, by a thousand or more of the Mexicans under Santa Anna—I have sustained a continued bombardment and cannonade for 24 hours and have not lost a man—the enemy has demanded a surrender at discretion, otherwise, the garrison are to be put to the sword, if the fort is taken—I have answered the demand with a cannon shot, and our flag still waves proudly from the walls—*I shall never surrender or retreat.* Then, I call on you in the name of Liberty, of patriotism, and everything dear to the American character, to come to our aid, with all dispatch—The enemy is receiving reinforcements daily and will no doubt increase to three or four thousand in four or five days. If this call is neglected, I am determined to sustain myself as long as possible and die like a soldier who never forgets what is due to his honor and that of his country—VICTORY OR DEATH.

WILLIAM BARRET TRAVIS
Lt. Col. comdt.

The Mexicans, the first day, and for a good deal of the second, did not completely encircle the Alamo. They left a gap on the east side, the side nearest to Washington-on-the-Brazos and to the American border. It is possible that they did this because they were so tired, for they had been moving fast for weeks and through the harshest kind of weather. It is more likely that they did it in the hope that some or even most of the Americans would take that opportunity to desert. If so, they were disappointed. The only person to go out through that gap in the investment was the boy who carried Travis' letter.[8]

Perfecto de Cos was out there in the Mexican camp, with all of his men. Under direct orders from his brother-in-law, who asked what after all was a promise given to a rebel, he had violated his parole.

The second night some of the men made a sally from the main gate, their objective being a group of small wooden houses or shacks too close for comfort. They dismantled as many of these as they had time for, firewood being precious, and the rest they put to the torch, lest they supply cover for the attackers.

The weather was cold and wet; the sky the color of a rat's back.

The tricolor was not the only Mexican thing in the Alamo. The defenders wore no hint of a uniform, though such officers as could get them had swords, and neither were there any insignia to indicate rank. Though there was no model, and some of the men wore floppety black felt hats, while a few, like Davy Crockett, wore coonskin caps with the tail hanging down behind, by far the most popular headgear within the walls was the *sombrero,* an eminently sensible hat for such a country. The besiegers, on the other hand, looked like green-clad West Point cadets without chin straps, for they wore white crossbelts and varnished high black hats, perhaps the silliest military headwear ever devised.

Mexicans were pouring up from the south every day. The four-pounders, with which they had been peppering the Alamo with little effect, day and night, no doubt for the purpose of rasping the defenders' nerves, now were augmented by twelve-pounders, guns that could take big bites out of that earth barrier. Twice, at night, the defenders made sallies in the hope of spiking these large pieces, but both times they were beaten off.

A great deal of cheering from the town, and a flapping of banners, told the defenders one afternoon that Antonio

Lopez de Santa Anna had arrived to take charge of the siege in person.

A more important arrival, in the eyes of the men inside, was on the night of March 1, when thirty-two volunteers from Gonzales appeared, on foot, at the main gate. A trigger-happy sentry had fired at them, and they were furious. Sure, they knew what they were doing! They knew that they did not stand one chance in a thousand of getting out of this place alive, but still they had come. They had heard of no other reinforcements.

This brought the total number of men within the walls to 187, including the sick.

The besiegers had left the east side only patrolled with occasional groups of horsemen, and it was through this space that the men from Gonzales had come; but now they closed the gap, and there were Mexicans and their little gray tents for as far as the eye could see. The ancient monastery was completely surrounded.

It was evident that the attack, when it came, would come from all sides at once.

The Mexicans were busy scouring the plain for wood—not just firewood, though they did use vast quantities of that, but sticks with which to make scaling ladders and fascines. Their engineers at last had succeeded in cutting off the water that ran through the irrigation ditches along the east and west walls, but it had rained a great deal and those ditches were filled with scummy mud, into which soldiers could sink. This was the reason for the fascines or bundles of sticks tied together. They would be tossed into those ditches just before the assault.

Meanwhile the twelve-pounders were hammering the wall to bits, chewing it up. The Mexicans had a few eighteen-pounders at work by this time too, and the north wall in particular had almost ceased to exist.

It was a bleak Sunday morning, March 6, a morning of

cruel wind, when the Alamo fell.

After thirteen days of preparation, the thing was over in a few minutes. The assault had been perfectly planned and was perfectly executed, a masterpiece of the military art. The little green soldiers in the high black hats never hesitated, and never met any real trouble.

Travis was in the northwest corner of the plaza, trying to turn around one of the old four-pounders, when he was shot down. Davy Crockett, at the west wall, had run out of powder and ball and so he clubbed with Betsy, grasping its hot barrel in his two hands, and went down swinging. Jim Bowie, his famous knife by his side, was in the hospital on the second floor of the barracks building. He must have given them a fight, as he had sworn to do, for his body was hideously slashed. He died as he had lived—hard.

Other patients in the hospital tried to hide beneath their blankets. It did them no good. They were hauled out and slaughtered.

When it was clear that the game was up, twenty-odd men dropped over what was left of the east wall and started to run across the plain. They were ridden down and skewered by lancers stationed there for that purpose.

Many of the defenders took refuge in the ground floor of the barracks building, a space that had once been the officers' quarters, a series of cell-like rooms, not connected with one another, each opening upon the plaza by means of a stout wooden door. They bolted those doors behind them— two or three in one room, five or six in the next.

This gave the Mexicans their only pause, but it was not much of a pause. They quickly wheeled around the captured four-pounders—there had not been time to spike them —and battered the doors down with cannonballs, one after the other. As each was blown to pieces, expert bayonet men rushed in. The defenders of the Alamo had no bayonets.

The bodies were stripped and piled like cordwood and

burned, the wind mercifully carrying the stink away.

They found one fellow two hours later, in a ditch out on the plain to the east, a ditch into which he had jumped or fallen, perhaps because he had sprained his ankle. They killed him.

CHAPTER

4

The Great Remembering

PANIC HIT TEXAS like a tornado. Women who suddenly found themselves to be widows gathered their children about them and started for the east in whatever vehicles were available—or often enough on foot. Men pushed past them, looking for their own wives. And there were chickens and pigs and a few cows. All of Texas was on the move, toward the safety of the Louisiana line, in a relentless rain.

There was no order; there was only unashamed fear, a mad wish to get to the States as soon as possible, at no matter whose cost.

This became known as the "Runaway Scrape."

The council had at last, and indisputably, created Sam Houston commander of the new Texan army—until this time his position had been a shaky one—and he was quick to organize a relief column. This column started for the Alamo March 7, the day after the monastery fell. It was soon learned what had happened, and the column turned back.

Men were deserting in droves, sometimes giving a brief notice first, more often just slipping away. But many would come back, with their guns, as soon as they had made sure that their wives and children were safe.

At no time did Houston have fewer than 450 men im-

SAM HOUSTON

mediately under him, and at no time did he have more than 1,400, but they came and went so fast that he could never be sure of the size of his own force. Moreover, sometimes captains or colonels theoretically under his orders would lead their men elsewhere, if they thought that he was being too timid—or too daring. It was, indeed, an army of generals, this amorphous mob. It could march in all directions at the same time.

Sam Houston (he seems never to have been called Samuel, not even by his various wives) was an extraordinary man, the prototype Texan. He was large, usually amiable, but had a fiery temper. He had more than once winged his man in duels, but he was willing to step outside and take his coat off with anybody who wanted to settle an argument in less formal fashion. Yet he could be diplomatic! He had been highly successful in his dealings with the Indians, among whom he had lived at one time—though handling Cherokees, it must be admitted, was not the same thing as handling Texans.

He was a major general of militia, and though not a

full-time professional soldier he had known plenty of experience in the field, and at this time was probably the best military man in Texas, not excepting His Excellency Antonio Lopez de Santa Anna.

Their methods were different. Santa Anna was aloof, arrogant, an enforcer of the strictest sort of discipline. Houston could sing along with his men, and he thought nothing of getting off his horse to put a shoulder to some wheel mired in the mud. Santa Anna believed in frightfulness, the war of terror; he believed in striking hard and savagely, burning and killing, showing no mercy, and he even encouraged his men to loot the homes of Mexicans, so as to make their passing more memorable. Santa Anna had been in Texas before, and he thought that he understood the Texan mind, for he had seen what cowards the border ruffians of his teen-age days were, and he assumed that they had not changed. Sam Houston knew better. Houston knew that cold-blooded killing might appall the Texans, but it would not deter them, for they were another breed of men from the semi-bandits young Lieutenant Santa Anna and Captain Santa Anna had faced so long ago.

Houston had been strongly opposed to the stand at the Alamo, though he was prompt to take advantage of its propaganda value afterward. Santa Anna would concentrate his units and strike one terrible blow, smashing the rebels, and thereafter he would *scatter* his forces in a series of violent mopping-up measures—that was the way he fought. Sam Houston, on the other hand, believed in backing away—at least until he had a decided advantage—and watching for the enemy to make a misstep. He thought that nothing west of the Colorado and perhaps not even anything west of the Brazos should be defended. He was much criticized for this, but he stuck to it.

Santa Anna did in fact break up his forces, assigning three generals each to a different army. So sure was he that the real part of the war was over, the glory-grabbing part, that he was prepared to go back to Mexico City and allow lesser personages to attend to the final details. He was dissuaded from this course only with difficulty.

Houston's rabble not only did not disperse, it kept getting bigger. This, Santa Anna could not understand.

Many of the Texans, for their part, had assumed that the war was over when Cos was defeated in the house-to-house fighting at San Antonio. Hadn't he given his promise to go back across the Rio Grande with all his men, never to return? So they went home—many, even most of them. For a time very few Texans—the thirty-two from Gonzales were exceptional—had been fighting for Texas; this was being done by outside volunteers. But now the old ones were coming back. "Remember the Alamo!" they were learning to shout. "Remember Goliad!"

Santa Anna conceived a plan to end the war in one fell swoop. The provisional government, originally based at Washington-on-the-Brazos, had retreated to Harrisburg, a hamlet on the San Felipe-Lynchburg road. Taking only a few hundred men, Santa Anna split his forces yet again and made a pounce upon Harrisburg. It was a bold move, characteristic of the man, but it failed, for the *politicos* had fled. As soon as he had been reinforced, Santa Anna sent another fast force, under Colonel Almonte, to tiny New Washington at the head of Galveston Bay, where he had heard that the so-called president of the provisional republic of Texas, David G. Burnet, lived. Almonte missed Burnet by minutes, but he did seize valuable supplies.

Santa Anna burned Harrisburg and prepared to go to Anahuac on the east side of Galveston Bay, from whence he could easily march up the line of the Trinidad River, cutting the Texans off from the Gulf and Louisiana at the same time. Thereafter they must either stand and fight—and he would ask nothing better—or fall like overripe plums into his basket.

The rain at last had ceased, though the ground remained soggy and the streams were running high and fast. The day of April 21 dawned clear, for a change; it was going to be hot and hazy. The two armies, each numbering about eight hundred men, were camped about three-quarters of a mile from one another in a roughly triangular cul-de-sac formed by the San Jacinto River, Buffalo Bayou, and Vince's Bayou. All of these bodies of water were high at their banks, and their edges were stripped with marshland. The rest, inside of that triangle, was prairie land stippled with live oaks all hung with Spanish moss.

Each knew that the other was there, though the camps were not in sight of one another; and Sam Houston knew, in addition, because of certain seized dispatches, that Santa Anna was expecting reinforcements under General Cos at any hour.

Santa Anna might then attack; but if instead he elected to retreat across one of the waterways, Houston was prepared to fall upon him from behind.

The reinforcements came in the middle of the morning, about 550 men, it was estimated. They looked dog-tired, scarcely able to stumble along. Houston tried to launch a rumor that they had really come from the regular Mexican camp, having been marched around an upswelling of the prairie, "an old dirty Mexican trick," but it is to be doubted that anybody was fooled. He might have saved himself the trouble. These men of his still were not very good at the manual of arms, and they talked back to their officers; but their spirit could not have been bettered. That they were to be outnumbered almost two to one did not dismay them. They were ready to fight their weight in wildcats, and more.

At about noon the staff officers asked the general if he would call a council of war. He consented. He had never done this before, it being his practice to keep plans to himself until the last moment.

There were four colonels and lieutenant colonels and two majors, besides a civilian, Thomas Rusk, the Texan secretary of war.

The question was: Should they attack or wait to be attacked?

The two junior officers, asked first, voted to attack. The senior officers, and the secretary, voted to sit tight. The Texans were in a good spot, they argued, and to throw raw militia, not equipped with bayonets, against trained troops on an open plain would be suicide.

Sam Houston thanked them, and dismissed them.

He sent Erastus ("Deaf") Smith—whom he always called "Mister E"—with another axman to chop down the bridge over Vince's Bayou. Deaf Smith grinned when he got that order, for he knew what it meant. The bridge over Vince's Bayou was the only way a defeated army, whether Texan or Mexican, could retreat in a hurry. In other words, this was to be a showdown.

The general had decided to strike.

He waited until the hour of the siesta. It was half-past three when at last they set forth through the live oaks, which cloaked this movement until the emergence. They had to be ordered not to sing.

Ahead of them, zealously handled by nine men each, went their whole artillery train, two six-pounders. These were excellent guns, brand-new, of cast iron, the gift of the people of Cincinnati. They had traveled far—down the Ohio, down the Mississippi, and across a large corner of the Gulf of Mexico—and they had not yet been fired. There were no balls for them, but the blacksmiths had manufactured canister of a sort by mixing sawed-up horseshoes with other bits and pieces of metal, and General Houston himself had contributed his saddle blanket to be cut into powder bags.

The men called these guns the Twin Sisters.

The Mexican camp was badly located, with swamp on one side, a thick morass behind. Some of the staff officers had pointed this out to Santa Anna—or were to say later that they had—but he was not a man you could argue with. Anyway, he seemed out of sorts. Perhaps he was ill? His health had never been dependable.

Cos's soldiers obviously were too tired to fight that day, so the President put the whole thing off and retired to his tent for a siesta.

No extra sentries had been posted, despite the nearness of the enemy, and no extra scouts sent out. On the side of the camp toward the Texans there had been erected a sort of breastwork made of boxes and crates and saddles, but it was a flimsy barrier.

Most of the men—perhaps all of Cos's, who had marched for more than thirty continuous hours—were following the example of their leader, and were asleep. Santa Anna seemed to have assumed that nobody would attack so late in the day. The big twelve-pounder, the army's pride, was not loaded. Horses were not saddled. Wash was hung out everywhere. Nothing was ready.

This was the scene upon which Houston's men, running out from the cover of the live oaks, burst like a bomb. Houston himself rode back and forth at the head of them, yelling, "Hold your fire! God damn it, *hold your fire!*" They would have time for only one volley, and it must be a close one to count.

Meanwhile the Twin Sisters were ripping holes through that sleazy breastwork.

There was scattered Mexican musket fire, but it was much too high. The Texans, bending over as they had been instructed to do, never wavered.

At sixty yards they were commanded to kneel and to fire. The Twin Sisters ceased to speak. The men started shouting.

"*Remember the Alamo!*"

They did not pause to reload but dashed through the breaches with clubbed guns or bowie knives.

The business that followed did not take more than twenty minutes—eighteen, by Sam Houston's own estimate. It has been called the Battle of San Jacinto, but it was more like a clash between two street gangs.
The Mexicans broke and ran, those who still could.
Santa Anna, in a blue linen dressing robe and red leather slippers, sprang out of his marquee, wringing his hands and shouting something that nobody could understand, but when an aide brought him a horse he mounted and rode off in the direction of Vince's Bayou. That was the direction most of them were taking.
General Castrillon, a good man, tried to organize some resistance, but he was shot in the head.
Colonel Almonte did get together some 350 to 400 unarmed fugitives outside of the camp, and hoisted a white flag, an action that probably saved their lives. Singly, they would have been hacked down.
Many of the Mexicans, far from offering any fight, dropped to their knees and spread their arms, crying: "Me no Alamo! Me no Alamo!" This helped some of them. Others it did not help.
The pursuit was mostly on foot, though some of the Texans did take Mexican horses on which to pursue Mexican soldiers. Soon the prairie for miles around was strewn with corpses. Vince's Bayou was the worst spot. When they found that the bridge was out scores of fugitives tried to swim or wade across—and didn't make it. The strip of water was literally clogged with drowned men, so that some of the few who did escape did so by walking across their dead comrades, a bridge of bodies.
It was to the credit of the Texan officers, and of Colonel Almonte, that there were 730 prisoners at the end of that bloody afternoon. Virtually all the rest of that force of about 1,560 men were dead or wounded, most of them dead.
The Texans really *had* remembered the Alamo.

CHAPTER

5

Hiss the Villain

THE PRISONERS OF COURSE expected to be killed. That was the way it was in war. When they had survived the night—and the morning of the twenty-second promised another chilly but bright day, another dry day—they were amazed; and they could only suppose that the gringos were waiting for full daylight so that their aim would be better. When they were given breakfast they were flabbergasted.

Their guards, the fierce men with the long knives, called angrily to them from time to time something they took to be: "Where's Santa Anna? Which one's Santa Anna?" They would shake their heads and mutter "Me no Alamo," though most of them were lying when they said that. It got so that the officers and even the noncoms surreptitiously removed their epaulettes and shoulder straps and other insignia of rank, each in fear that he might be mistaken for the President-General.

All that day they were not killed. They could hardly believe it.

Among the supplies seized were two hundred horses; privates and sergeants were given their pick of these and sent out in small squads to scour the surrounding plain and especially to poke into the bogs and gullies in search of any

Mexican, alive or dead, who might be thought to resemble Santa Anna. Houston, lying under a live oak in great pain—his left leg had been shattered just above the ankle, and the surgeon feared that lockjaw might set in—was troubled about Santa Anna. He had reason to know that General Filisola with the main body of the Mexicans, something between two thousand and three thousand men, was less than fifty miles away, and he could well believe that Filisola had been sent for and already was on his way. If Santa Anna took up with him, all the fighting at San Jacinto would have been in vain, all the loot would be lost, and Texan independence might become again no more than a dim hope.

One of the search squads was led by Sergeant James A. Sylvester, who late in the afternoon sent the others back to camp with a single prisoner, while he remained on the prairie to do a little more scouring.

The prisoner was a polite man with a quiet voice. They had found him at the edge of a field near the ruins of Vince's Bridge. He had tried to hide, but when they hailed him he came trembling to them. He wore an outlandish combination of not too clean country clothes, and he protested that he was no more than a private who had got those clothes from a deserted farmhouse. He could or would speak no English, but one of the privates, Joel Robison, spoke a little Spanish and could interpret. When they examined this prisoner more carefully they saw that he was wearing under his smock a beautiful shirt in which were set golden studs. They taxed him with this, and he broke down and confessed that he was not a private at all but an aide to General Santa Anna. They took him into camp, and were about to release him among the other prisoners—when those others put on a strange act. They began to uncover, to salute, to bow. *"El Presidente!"* they cried. *"El Presidente!"* So they took him before General Houston, to whom he made a bow, introducing himself as General Antonio Lopez de Santa Anna,

President of Mexico. A little later, when the useful Colonel Almonte had been brought in as an interpreter, Santa Anna added that now the *norteamericanos* would have a chance to be generous to the vanquished.

"You should have thought of that at the Alamo," said Sam Houston.

But Houston was gracious. He ordered that Santa Anna's gorgeous marquee be erected for him again, all its furnishings intact. Santa Anna felt better when he had gone to his medicine chest and taken out an opium pill, which he chewed—it helped his nerves.

The dirtiest part of the whole business was left to the mass burial squads of the twenty-second. They had to work at it all day, for though the nights were cold the sun was hot in the daytime, and already those bodies were rotting and the stink in the nearby camp was almost unbearable.

Among the loot was a treasure chest with $12,000 in gold. Two thousand dollars of this the men voted to give to the small but spunky Texas navy. The rest they split up evenly among themselves, and it came to approximately $7.50 a man. That was all they ever got for that campaign.

There were a good many of the men—they might even have constituted a majority—who would have liked more than that—they would have liked Santa Anna's blood, and they were vociferous about it. Sam Houston, who was in agony all this while, had to use every bit of his popularity to save the life of his illustrious prisoner.

There under the live oak *El Presidente* proposed that they frame an armistice. Houston replied that he had no authority, as a military man, to do this: it was up to the civilian authorities. Santa Anna said that he did not like dealing with civilians, and Houston had no comment to make on this.

At last they drew up two totally illegal treaties, one for public display, the other a secret treaty, though the differences between them were trifling. Both, in effect, promised on Santa Anna's part that he would order all Mexican troops out of Texas and that when he returned to Mexico himself he would work for full Texan independence and a formal end of the war; while the new republic pledged itself to see that he was sent to Vera Cruz as soon as this was "convenient."

Santa Anna thereupon sat down and wrote to Vincenza Filisola ordering him to leave Texas with all his men and not come back. This, delivered promptly, put Filisola in a spot. If he obeyed, he would almost certainly be called back to the capital to face charges, but if he did not obey he would be making an enemy of a highly slippery political operator, a man who did not believe in forgiveness, and who might any month now be back in power. It meant a court-martial one way or the other, and Urrea advised him to disobey; but at last he decided to withdraw as far as Monterey, south of the Rio Grande.[9]

This retreat did not dull the clamor for *El Presidente*'s neck. There was wild talk about rushing his lodgings and hauling him out and lynching him, and undoubtedly there were many private assassination plans. The situation was made worse when Sam Houston took off for New Orleans, the surgeons fearing not only for his leg but for his very life. However, he was soon back, limping but as bluff as ever, and he was elected the first President of the Republic of Texas, in which capacity he conceived himself to be sole keeper of the distinguished prisoner and arranged for him to be sent by schooner to New Orleans.

Again, there was a barrier. Santa Anna boarded a schooner at Velasco, at the mouth of the Brazos, and he was in his cabin and had just finished inditing a graceful if unexpected little note to the soldiers of the Texas army, congratulating them on their intrepidity and thanking them for their understanding, when the vessel was boarded by a lot of newly arrived volunteers from the States. These youngsters, finding themselves cheated of glory by the sudden appearance of peace, demanded the dictator's head. They were very emphatic about it. The least that should be done, they said, was a public trial—and inevitable conviction.

It was touch and go for several days there, and Sam Houston had to use all his influence at long distance before the schooner at last was allowed to sail with a badly shaken Santa Anna. Colonel Almonte was with him, as were three civilian officials.

Antonio Lopez de Santa Anna had conceived a desire to visit Washington, D.C., and to meet President Andrew Jackson, whom he greatly admired from afar.

The party moved without fanfare, for there was always the fear of assassination. They went up the Mississippi, up the Ohio as far as Louisville, which they reached on Christmas Day of 1836, and there they stayed for almost two weeks while Santa Anna was being treated for a severe cold. The rest of the trip was made in a couple of chartered coaches, and there was never any violence involved in it.

Mexico City had duly informed the State Department in Washington that Mexico would not be bound by any treaties General Santa Anna might make when he was out of the country, but this did not prevent him from getting at least one talk with President Jackson, and he might have had two. It was all unofficial and not a matter of record.

It was President Jackson's wish that the United States purchase Texas from Mexico, which should be glad to get money for something she had irretrievably lost. The States had not yet ceremoniously recognized the existence of the new republic, and though the idea of annexation had been broached nothing had been done about this. Nor did anything decisive come out of the conversation or conversations between the two presidents. Andrew Jackson was nearing the end of his second term in the White House and in a few weeks he would cease to be President, so that he was not eager to set a policy that might embarrass his successor. He seems, however, to have thought well of Antonio Lopez de Santa Anna, for he sent him home in a frigate of the United States Navy, *Pioneer*.

The homecoming at Vera Cruz was anything but enthusiastic. Indeed, the crowd was in an ugly mood and the former hero might have met with the violence he had avoided in the United States had it not been for the behavior of the American commanding naval officer, who, in dress uniform, went ashore with his passenger and stayed close to him all the way up to the main Santa Anna residence in Jalapa.

There was a national election soon after this, and Santa Anna got only two electoral votes. His old enemy Bustamante won easily.

This did not faze Santa Anna. He was comfortable, he was rich, he could wait.

It was the so-called "French Pastry War" that saved him.

The proprietor of a French restaurant near Mexico City, one Rémontel, had been visited by a group of high-spirited officers on the eve of their departure for Texas—Santa Anna's own men—who, having made a night of it, locked him in his room and ransacked the place, taking, among other things, all of the pastry. There was nothing unusual about this in itself; but Rémontel had learned, as had other Frenchmen, Americans and Britons, that the Mexican courts were unabashedly venal and made no pretense of dispensing justice, so he gave his claim to the French ambassador, who had hundreds of other similar ones. They came to about $600,000 in all, none of which, it soon became apparent, the Mexican government had any intention of paying. Things took a different turn, and the tut-tutting was abruptly ended, when a French fleet sailed into the harbor at Vera Cruz and demanded that the $600,000 be paid immediately. When this was not done—there was, as usual, no money in the treasury—the French proceeded to batter to pieces the great fort San Juan de Ulúa, sometimes called the Gibraltar of America, a process watched with interest by the skipper of a noncombatant vessel that just happened to be on hand, Commander David Farragut, U.S.N. Mexico, furious, declared war. Santa Anna was called in. Wasn't he an expert on chasing foreigners out of the country? Next to the Spaniards the French were the most numerous aliens in Mexico; and France, a monarchy at the moment, looked with no notable favor upon a republican Mexico, a state she had been one of the last to recognize.

Santa Anna negotiated a cease-fire, to which there was a strict time limit, but before he could think of what else to do the French admiral Baudin had the bright thought that he would be in a better bargaining position if he held, as General Houston once had, the *corpus* of Santa Anna himself; and with this in mind he sent a kidnapping party ashore. They made a lot of noise breaking into Santa Anna's town house, and he escaped in his underclothes. In a wood outside of the city he organized a resistance party, which dashed to the Vera Cruz waterfront just in time to be too late. The French, reembarking in their boats, were all unscratched. As though in contempt, they fired one shot from a small fieldpiece at the oncharging Mexicans, Santa Anna at their head. It killed the horse and it shattered the rider's left leg.

That was a momentous shot. Santa Anna played the leg for all it was worth, and a little more. It had to be amputated, and he sent it to the government at Mexico City, together with a fantastic report in which he claimed to have beaten off a fierce French attack, killing many of the invaders, including Admiral Baudin. It was preposterous, but it worked. The government built a special mausoleum in which to inter the severed leg, meanwhile erecting yet another statue of Antonio Lopez de Santa Anna. The French eventually got everything they had demanded, but before this happened Santa Anna somehow—a hero again, he knew how to manage these affairs—had become President.

He had almost certainly promised Andrew Jackson that he would work in Mexico for the sale of Texas to the United States: otherwise, he would hardly have got that frigate. The first thing he did when he became *El Presidente* once again was vow on his sacred honor as a soldier that he would bring Texas back into the Mexican fold.

What were you going to do with a man like that?

CHAPTER

6

The Cut-Ups

EIGHTEEN-FORTY was the damnedest presidential election in the history of the United States.
The political situation was confusing, to start with. The bits and pieces of the old Federalist party had long since fallen apart, even in New England, and the men who had followed Jefferson into power in 1800—the republicans, as they were called then, later the republican-democrats, later still the democrat-republicans, and more recently, and officially, the Democrats, spelled with a capital "D"—for a long time had been firmly in the saddle, without any mentionable opposition. Their strongest trump card was the "Old Hero of The Hermitage," Andrew Jackson, a rough man for anyone to face, a lank man with wavy hair, with a pump-handle chin, a prodigious fighter, impatient of opposition. But even Jackson, though his personal popularity remained undimmed, would not venture to break the limit-of-two-terms tradition set by Washington, Jefferson, Madison, and Monroe, and when the end of his eighth year as President had passed he bowed out—first, however, naming his successor.
This was Martin Van Buren—short, plump, bald on top,

the son of a tavern keeper of humble Dutch ancestry. Van Buren was a successful New York lawyer, a self-made gentleman, sometimes called the Fox, an animal he did resemble slightly, with his sharp small eyes and his fringe of reddish whiskers now flecked with gray, and sometimes the Wizard or the Magician, from his ability to pull almost any kind of rabbit out of almost any political hat. People, somehow, did not trust Martin Van Buren. They thought he was a weathervane, a me-tooer. It was true that he had matured, in Washington, under the protective shade of the Old Hero who cast a stupendous shadow, and true too that, repelled by the barbarity of the Jackson years, he had prettied up the White House, expecting more of the servants there, so that his enemies accused him of putting on airs, a deadly sin. It was even said that he wore a corset and used cologne, but there is no proof of this.

Van Buren was unanimously nominated at the Democratic National Convention of 1836, a convention packed with Federal officeholders, and he won the election readily enough, despite the fact that his running mate, insisted upon by the Old Hero, was Colonel Richard M. Johnson, a man who had lived with a mulatto woman, by whom he had two acknowledged daughters, conduct frowned upon in the South. "Little Van" made a good President, proving, unexpectedly, that he had a mind of his own. Against the howls of employers that it would spoil the American workman, for instance, he decreed that all those employed upon Federal projects should enjoy the benefits of the ten-hour day. Yet his administration had been plagued by two separate financial panics, for which of course it was blamed, and he faced 1840 with trepidation.

The convention gave no trouble. Old Hickory, far away in retirement, nevertheless was a power; and Little Van himself was an expert at rigging delegations. But now he faced real opposition—the Whigs.

This was not so much a political party as it was a conglomeration of hates, a congress of dislikes. The Republican National Party, made up mostly of shards from the shattered Federalist pitcher, had attracted to itself all manner of anti's, and had been showing considerable strength in recent years, though it still was weak in the South. The Whigs—the name itself had been formally used for them in the 1834 campaign in New York State and was already accepted all over the nation—had certain somewhat hazy goals, but their only *real* purpose was to get the Democrats out.

There were many possible candidates when the Whigs went into convention at Harrisburg, Pennsylvania, in December of 1839, with twenty-two states (Georgia, South Carolina, Arkansas, and Tennessee were not there) represented by 254 delegates. There was that enormous pouter-pigeon General Winfield Scott, who had the New York delegation in his pocket—or thought he did. There was Daniel Webster, majestic as a volcano and almost as noisy, but he had no following outside of New England and he had been the paid lawyer of the Bank of the United States, an organization the Whigs professed to abhor. There was General William Henry Harrison, of whom the most that could be said was that nobody had anything against him. And there was Henry Clay.

Clay, from Kentucky, was incomparably the ablest man in the party, head and shoulders above any of the others in ability. He had behind him a distinguished career in the United States Senate. He was popular in the West and even well thought of in the South, where the Whigs did not hope to pick up many votes. Though he was already famous for his assertion that he would rather be right than President—a remark he himself was to say had been "applauded beyond its merit"—he would have liked to be both.

There were a few points upon which Henry Clay did not seem to be "available," but they were minor points. He was a slave owner, though not a large one, in a land where the abolitionists were a growing group. He was a duellist;

and duelling, at least in the East, since the Hamilton-Burr affair almost half a century before, had been looked upon as a disgrace. He liked his liquor, but he could hold it, and he had been known to play for high stakes in poker. (When his wife was asked if she didn't worry about his gambling she replied: "Why should I? He almost always wins.") Worst of all, he was a Mason, and there was a great deal of anti-Masonry feeling in the country just then.

"If my name creates any obstacle to union and harmony, away with it, and concentrate upon some individual more acceptable to all branches," he had written to the convention; but when the delegates did exactly that, passing him by for General Harrison, he was furious and paced the floor, swearing violently.

For Vice President, after four other men had refused the honor, the Whigs nominated John Tyler of Virginia, a man who stood for almost everything that they opposed. They did this, no doubt, on the assumption that Harrison, who was sixty-six, was immortal.

There was no platform. Why get involved in serious discussions? The Whigs had a better plan.

Texas, recognized as an independent republic, still wanted to get into the Union, but Texas had slavery and many of the northern statesmen feared to see slavery extended, the power of the South in Congress increased. The Whigs at least ignored the issue of annexation. They went further. They ignored *all* of the issues.

A friend of Clay (who, by the way, got over his rage and took the stump), when he heard of the nomination, remarked that if William Henry Harrison had $2,000 a year and plenty of hard cider he would be perfectly content to spend the rest of his days in his log cabin studying moral philosophy. That this had been meant to be in part fond, that it had been said by a Whig, made no difference. When it was published in a Baltimore paper the Whigs picked it up instantly, implying—though they never said this outright

—that it had been said by a dirty Democrat who meant to traduce General Harrison. What was the matter with living in a log cabin, that most American of all houses, howsoever humble it might be? What was the matter with being poor, a farmer not too proud to work in his own fields? If it came to that, what was the matter with hard cider, a drink certainly more appropriate to a Presidential nominee than the fancy French wines that Little Van preferred?

If they had been able to make themselves heard, the Democrats might have retorted that so far from being a lowly farmer William Henry Harrison was the scion of an aristocratic Virginia family, one of the FFV's—the Charles City County Harrisons, not the Tidewater Harrisons—and the son of Benjamin Harrison, onetime Governor of Virginia, first chairman of the Continental Congress that had adopted the Declaration of Independence and himself a signer. The son had been given a classical education, and had spent his life either in the army or as a Federal officeholder; he had never been a farmer; and though in 1840 the family fortunes were not as considerable as they had previously been, he drew $6,000 a year, which would permit any man to live in ease, even in luxury, as clerk of the Cincinnati courts, a sinecure. He did not dwell in a log cabin, nor was the log cabin an American invention, for it had been brought to America by Swedes, and the English settlers at Jamestown and at Plymouth had never even heard of such a structure.[10] General Harrison lived in a large comfortable house in Ohio, a house surrounded by widespread gardens, but no farmlands. A hut not unlike the Swedish log cabin might once have formed the nucleus of this house, a sort of engineer's shack later to be enclosed in the whole; but if so, William Henry Harrison had had no part of it. What his tastes in intoxicants might have been is not a matter of record, but he could well afford French wines and brandy.

But—why drag in all those dry facts? It was much more fun to remind folks that General Harrison had been in command of the American forces that routed some Indians at a place called Tippecanoe, a place most voters until then had never even heard of, and to emphasize this by carrying canoes in all the parades.

For the Whigs, at this time, invented the campaign parade. There had been some rather solemn marches on the part of solemn high-hatted men who wished to assert their solemn belief in a cause, but never, oh never! anything like this.

Twenty thousand turned out at Columbus, Ohio, marching eight abreast. Some of the floats depicted canoes, more depicted log cabins. There was a great deal of cheering, a great deal of undignified singing.

What has caused the great commotion, motion, motion,
Our country through?
It is the ball a-rolling on
For Tippecanoe and Tyler too.

and:

Van, Van
Is a used-up man.

After Columbus there came parades in Dayton, Syracuse, Boston, New York, Philadelphia, Baltimore, each one bigger than the last, with scores of log cabin floats. Those that were given at night were featured by red fire, used now for the first time.

Some of the floats were elaborate, real smoke coming out of the chimney of the log cabin, a coonskin nailed to the door, or a live coon tethered on the roof, and always with the latchstring all the way out to commemorate General Harrison's farewell speech to his soldiers, when he told them that the latchstring would always be out at his house for them. Usually, too, there was a barrel, on which would be painted, lest there be any mistake, HARD CIDER.

Occasionally, for a laugh, there would be a float depicting Martin Van Buren, the President of the United States, always a pale, effete little man in a ruffled shirt, who wallowed in silken cushions, a glass of champagne in one hand, the bottle in the other.

"Go it, Tip!" the faithful would shout. "Go it, Ty!"

It was no use for the Democrats to try to arrange debates on the tariff or the one-term issue. "Harrison, two dollars a day, and roast beef!" would be yelled back at them; or else the irrepressible Whigs once again would burst into song, rendering perhaps the "Log Cabin Waltz" or the "Log Cabin Quick Step," both hits, or:

Oh know ye the farmer of Tippecanoe?
The gallant old farmer of Tippecanoe?
With an arm that is strong and a heart that is true,
The man of the people is Tippecanoe.

Van Buren won only seven of the twenty-six states, and Harrison got a plurality of 174 electoral votes. The popular vote was much closer—1,275,016 to 1,129,102—but nevertheless Van-Van-the used-up-man was out and the Gallant Farmer was in.

They had kept the candidate pretty well under wraps during the campaign, and though he did talk a few times in public he never said anything. "General Mum" the Democrats called him. However, he was permitted to write his own inauguration speech, which Henry Clay severely cut. Still, it took an hour and forty minutes to deliver, and *it*, too, said nothing. Perhaps the effort was too much for the general, who by that time was sixty-seven, the oldest man ever to be elected President of the United States. He was also the shortest-lived President.[11] Exactly a month after the inauguration, April 4, he died of pneumonia.

The Whigs, the cheers dying on their lips, were faced then with John Tyler, an ardent annexationist.

CHAPTER

7

Blood out of a Dream

INCIDENTS MAY NOT in themselves lead to war, but it is certain that the road to war is lined with them—on both sides.

The people of Texas, like those of Mexico, were emotional, easily moved. They were volatile. They were quick-tempered, explosive.

By the constitution of the new republic its president could not succeed himself in office, and after Sam Houston's term had run out Mirabeau Buonaparte Lamar was elected to replace him. Here was a poet, slim, fiery, with long wavy yellow hair, accipitrine facial features, and a fanatical fondness for dreams. A dashing cavalry officer, a war hero, he believed that Texas was quite capable of standing on her own feet and he disapproved of annexation.

Not only did he believe that Texas could and should stand alone, he thought that she could expand, gloriously, to the west and to the north, an empire. She could stretch herself to the Pacific. He was intoxicated by this prospect, and when he became president he proposed to do something about it.

He asked the Texas Congress for funds to raise and equip a trading expedition to Sante Fe, some 1,500 miles away, and when Congress refused he raised the money from the treasury himself somehow, using methods that were illegal but certainly not venal.

He insisted that this expedition was to be a peaceful one, purely commercial in its nature, though it was to be under the command of a brigadier general and include five companies of infantry, 265 men in all. The soldiers, the flamboyant Lamar said, were only to protect the wagon train —twenty-two wagons, and they were large ones—from Indians. One of the nonmilitary members of this curious party was George Wilkins Kendall, editor of the New Orleans *Picayune*, who was to act as its historian.

This was in 1841. There was nothing secret about the business, and the Mexican government knew of it well in advance and had notified the governor of New Mexico province, a very fat man named Armijo.

The expedition started out like a picnic, a gay hunting trip. There was an air of festivity about it. The wagons were filled with trade goods and also with copies of a proclamation, in English and in Spanish, boisterously issued by President Lamar, a proclamation in which he invited all his dear friends in Santa Fe to join with the Texans and be one big happy family of brothers. It did not occur to Mirabeau Buonaparte Lamar that the Mexicans might frown upon this proclamation, and even might, suspicious persons that they were, esteem it treason.

The holiday atmosphere evaporated. The way was all desert, bitterly cold at night, scorchingly hot in the daytime. Their livestock were soon depleted, so that they had to depend upon dried rations, while thirst was a demon clinging to each back. Their horses were cut out by cunning Indians, and their shoes, from walking, wore through. In rags, they were reduced to eating lizards and snakes.

Their Mexican guide, after leading them by a circuitous route to the worst place he could think of, deserted one night (he was a spy in Santa Anna's pay) and doubtless made his own way to Santa Fe to announce their arrival.

When at last they got to that capital and were met with a strong force of regulars they could offer no fight, for they could scarcely stand. They were thrown into a prison on starvation rations. Several who attempted to escape were beaten, then shot; all of the others were forced to witness these acts.

At last they were started on a march to Mexico City, two thousand miles away. The first part of this, as far as El Paso, was sheer hell. They were in the charge of a sadistic captain named Salezar, who only dribbled food to them, never covered them, and from time to time, simply for his own entertainment, made them trot on the double. When anybody died from exhaustion, as several did, his body was not buried but only left by the side of the trail, though his ears were dutifully cut off for the sake of the record.

Eventually what was left of them was locked in a medieval-type fortress, Perote, on the highway between Mexico City and Vera Cruz. After El Paso, where they were treated with kindness, and where the commanding military officer reproved Salezar for his senseless cruelties, the going had been much easier, though never a romp. But the damage, by that time, was done. These were highly articulate men, most of them, and when they wrote home what they mostly wrote about was that horrible march from Santa Fe to El Paso.

Their letters were tinder. Not only all of Texas but all of the United States as well was aflame with indignation. Even the Alamo, even Goliad, had not caused such cries of rage. The Texas Congress went so far as to declare war on Mexico, all unmindful of the fact that Mexico and Texas already *were* at war. Though Sam Houston, back in the presidency again, vetoed this, the Congress passed it over his veto—but the Congress, the two houses of which were at odds with one another, never could agree on war appropriations.

That massive military expedition to put down Texas, though often threatened, never seemed to materialize since Santa Anna was too busy putting down revolts nearer to the capital; but a good-sized Mexican force was kept in a threatening position near the Rio Grande. Some 1,400 of these men under General Rafael Vásquez made a hit-and-run raid on San Antonio the foggy night of March 5, 1842, and scampered away, unscathed, with about a hundred prisoners. Later that same year, September 20, a similar force under Colonel Adrian Woll did the same thing in the same place, bagging, this time, the judge, all members of a jury panel, and three Congressmen-lawyers, one of them the acting governor. These swelled the hostages at Perote, where the dungeons already were full.

Both of these raids were made on San Antonio, a town notable only for sentimental reasons, not at all for military reasons. The capital of the republic would have been a more reasonable target, but it may be that the Mexicans were not certain which town *was* the capital. The Texans themselves did not seem to be. In the few years of independence this had been moved from Washington-on-the-Brazos to Harrisburg, to Morgan's Point, to Galveston, to Columbia, to Houston, to Austin, to Houston again, and back to Washington, the town of its birth.

Pressure was being brought to bear on President Houston to order an invasion of Mexico, even storm Mexico City, though how he could do this with no war chest was never explained. He did send out one expedition of about 750 men under General Somerville to cross the Rio Grande in a simple show of force, camp a few days, and then return. Not all of the eager-eyed youngsters who still poured in from the States looking for a fight were interested in freedom and the right to a trial by jury. Some were, frankly, interested in booty; and Somerville, through no fault of his own, had more than his share of such. When they camped near Laredo, a town on the east bank of the river but largely populated by Mexicans, the men stripped shops and houses unconscionably. Somerville made them return most of the stuff that they had stolen, but two hundred of the more decent ones quit in disgust and went home. Somerville took the others across the river, and camped for a few days, as he had been ordered to do, but when he started them back about 360 refused to go. These, under a couple of captains they had elected themselves, attacked the west bank town of Mier, where they were encircled by a large force of converging Mexican regulars. The fighting was fierce for three days and three nights, but at last the Texans surrendered. On direct orders from the commander-in-chief, *El Presidente*, the survivors were decimated, literally—that is, they drew, blind, from a pot in which there were black beans and white beans, nine times as many white as black, and everybody who drew a black bean was shot, all at once, not one at a time. It was a messy procedure. Afterward the men who were left were marched to Perote, where they were imprisoned.

Angry words echo for a long while; instead of dying they sometimes swell. The Mexican minister of foreign affairs, one Bocanegra, an excitable person, gave to the local press a searing statement in which he accused the United States government of abetting and even inspiring the various armed parties that were still slipping into Texas. The minister, no doubt in order to curry favor with the public, had used exceedingly strong language; but since this was not an official paper it did not need to be officially answered, and in the ordinary course of events it would have been put aside as just another instance of bad taste. However, an American consul sent a copy of it to a friend of his, Commodore Thomas Ap Catesby Jones, an officer of Welsh background, a War of 1812 hero, who was the commander of the Pacific fleet of the United States Navy. Jones lay in the harbor of Callao in southwestern South America, and in that same harbor at the same time were a couple of British warships, which Jones was eyeing askance. This was the first mail Commodore Jones had received in half a year, and when he read the minister's statement he simply could not believe that war had not broken out between Mexico and the United States—no minister would say such a thing, otherwise; and no nation would permit it to go unrebuked. In the same mail Commodore Jones found a Boston newspaper in which it was stated positively that Mexico and Great Britain had signed an agreement ceding California, or at least a base in California, to Britain in the event of a war between Mexico and the United States.

Nineteen out of twenty Americans believed that Great Britain had been secretly dealing with Mexico for a Pacific port, and Thomas Ap Catesby Jones was no exception. A clipping from a Mexico City paper containing a fiery statement by the minister of foreign affairs, combined with the fact that just at that time the two British warships hauled out of Callao, making a course due north, settled Jones's mind for him. (Actually, they went to the Marquesas.) If any nation was going to get a chunk of California it must be his own. He called in his shore leave parties, hoisted his canvas, and set out for the north. That was September 7, 1842, a Wednesday.

Monterey was a long trip, six weeks. The skipper used much of that time in the writing and polishing of two turgid documents, an address to his faithful tars before going into battle, and a proclamation to the people of Monterey announcing the annexation of all California by the United States. Each, in his own eyes, was a masterpiece. Each was polysyllabic, bombastic, long, and desperately in earnest. Commodore Jones really made the eagle scream when he wrote.

They reached Monterey October 19, and everything

seemed quiet. Some fishermen they had picked up near the entrance of the harbor were asked about the progress of the war. *What* war? They didn't know nothing about no war.

Unabashed, Jones went on in with his little fleet—the frigate *United States* and the sloop-of-war *Cyane*—and formally summoned the garrison to surrender.

The soldiers of the garrison, all twenty-nine of them, were delighted to comply, and couldn't turn in their guns fast enough. They would no longer have to go through the motions of knocking some of the rust off those nine ancient cannons, which could not have been fired safely even if there was any powder; they would no longer have to stand guard duty; they could just sleep all day. Of course they surrendered.

Jones went ashore the following morning with ceremony, surrounded by Marines, to view his conquest. He caused the Mexican tricolor to be lowered from the flagpole in the plaza, and the Stars and Stripes run up in its place. He read his proclamation, which must have impressed any there who could understand English. Then he returned in triumph to his ship.

A Yankee businessman who ran a store in Monterey came to him with a newspaper dated much later than the paper Jones had seen in Callao. This was the third day, Friday, and still there was no sign of war. Monterey snoozed.

The paper, indeed, made it clear that there *wasn't* any war; and Jones was understandably irked. But he played the gentleman. He went ashore and apologized to the mayor and to the commanding officer of the garrison; he woke up and released from custody the soldiers; he caused the Stars and Stripes to be lowered, the Mexican flag to be run up, and he commanded that a full salute be fired to the latter from the *United States;* after which he sailed away.

The governor of California, one Micheltorena, had run inland, where he composed a furious letter addressed to

Jones, calling him everything under the sun and promising to cut him and all his men to pieces right way. He sent a copy of this letter to his superior in Mexico City (or perhaps he sent the original: Commodore Jones was to attest that he never received any such missive), who promptly turned it over to the local papers, which were always glad to get anti-Yanqui material.

If Jones had made a fool of himself, so had Micheltorena. The whole affair was to prove embarrassing to both sides, and nothing really came of it; but undoubtedly it deepened the belief of the Mexicans that there was a widespread *norteamericano* plot against them. Jones, they muttered, had only jumped the gun.

CHAPTER

8

The First Dark Horse

THE WHIGS HAD REACHED a new low in vulgarity with their campaign of 1840, and the Democrats were to reach a new low in smoke-filled hotel-room techniques with their 1844 national convention.

National conventions were new things. The *politicos* had yet to learn what delightful avenues of connivance they could open, what vistas of dealing and double-dealing. They were to learn at Baltimore. It was a revelation.

Both major parties had chosen the Maryland city for their conventions—a coincidence, the first time this had happened.

The Whig convention, to nobody's amazement, was to prove a shoo-in, a love feast. Henry Clay was nominated by acclaim, and only four ballots were taken to pick his running mate, Theodore Frelinghuysen of New Jersey. Clay had recently written a letter to a national publication, a letter in which he said that he could see no reason for annexing Texas and running the terrible risk of causing a split in the Union. This was to hurt him, and badly, but the wound did not show at the time of the first convention in Baltimore, early in May, where even the great Daniel Webster—and there was no love lost between these oratorical prima donnas [12]—thundered his praise.

With the Democrats it was different. Van-Van was by no means a used-up man, as he had been proving for four years. He had enjoyed himself in the White House and had a hankering to go back. With the perseverance of a mole he had for a long time been lining up delegates, and at the time of the descent upon Baltimore he had a majority of them in his pocket. A majority, however, might not be enough. In its first two national conventions the Democratic party had decreed that a two-thirds vote was needed for nomination, but in the third, the latest, 1840, it had agreed that a majority would suffice. Now the enemies of Van Buren were out to get the opening session of the convention to declare for a return to the two-thirds rule. This was the biggest problem that he faced.

Van Buren, like Clay, had written for publication a letter arguing that annexation might bring about a disruption of the Union and so should be avoided. These letters had been issued at the same time, causing many to contend that they were the result of collusion, a move to evade a troublesome problem by agreeing, in unison, not to look at it. This is conceivable, though the men were not in the same place at the time, Van Buren being in Old Kinderhook,[13] Clay in Raleigh, North Carolina. Little Van stuck to his resolution and never tried to hedge on it, as Clay was to try to do, for Clay decided, after a while, that annexation might not be such a bad thing if it could be accomplished "without dishonor, without war, upon the common consent of the Union, upon just and fair terms."

There was no lack of other aspirants. It was unthinkable that the party would nominate "His Accidency," President Tyler, after he had gone over to the Whigs, who now wanted no part of him; but he was talking about starting a third party, and he was an avowed annexationist: "Tyler and Texas," indeed, was the rallying cry of his followers.

Granitic old John Calhoun, "the sleepless guardian of slavery,"[14] would still have liked the prize, but he had built the Southern cause into a sort of Spinozan religio-philosophy that was well beyond the brush of argument, and all Northerners and most Westerners dreaded regionalism like the Devil. Lewis Cass of Michigan was prominently mentioned, and so were Silas Wright of New York, though perhaps he drank too much, Commodore Charles Stewart and James Buchanan of Pennsylvania, and R. M. ("Old Dick") Johnson, despite that dusky mistress who was dead now but whose ghost haunted him politically.

Cass, the strongest of these possible candidates, was all for annexation.

There was a colonial American political expression, "out of doors," which meant quiet person-to-person argument off the floor of the legislature or other lawmaking body. A man who might never occupy his chair in the chamber, or even *have* such a chair, and who never raised his voice in formal debate, but who was a shrewd operator in the lobbies and corridors—such a man was said to be a worker "out of doors." It is not likely that there was *literally* much political haggling out of doors when the Democrats got together in Baltimore—the weather would not have permitted it—but *figuratively* the city seethed.

Monday, May 27, was to be the opening day, and delegates and alternates began pouring into Baltimore from nearby Washington early (practically all of them were senators or congressmen), so that by Saturday every hotel room—and every barroom—was occupied.

Sunday the preconvention dickering really got under way. What a pleading, whispering, coaxing! What gnashing of teeth and shaking of fists, while deals were made in all directions, and delegates were dropped and swapped and shoved around! That was a day of torrential rains, of thunder and lightning and high howling wind; but the tumult in the streets was as nothing compared with that in the restaurants, taverns, and committee rooms. Nobody had ever known anything like it. Some few were disgusted, but most of the politicians took to this activity like ducks to water, delighting in it.

Monday morning Nature's storm had subsided, but Man's had only just begun. There was an immense crowd in Gay Street before the Odd Fellows' Hall, where the convention was to be held, and no delegate got to his seat unbuttonholed.

The stop-Van fanatics got off to a sensational start when, before all of the Van Burenites had reached the floor —some of that heavy jostling in the crowd outside might have been directed—they railroaded through a motion to make Hendrick B. Wright of Pennsylvania president of the convention. Wright, a bullish person with Stentor's voice, accepted the honor with undignified alacrity, immediately calling for a motion to restore the two-thirds vote requirement. Cave Johnson of Tennessee, an alert Van Buren man, objected, calling for the posting of an official roster of delegates before any such motion was voted upon. Wright tried to gavel him down, but he persisted and he carried his point. There was an adjournment until the middle of the afternoon, when the better prepared Van Buren forces tried to put through a motion that voting should be by unit rule. This brought about an hysterical debate, lasting well into the night, and the matter was still unsettled at adjournment. Next morning, thanks in large part to the chairman's gavel and the strength of his lungs, the unit rule motion was voted down, 148 to 118. It would be two-thirds, then.

There were 266 votes, so that 134 would constitute a majority, but 177 would be needed for a two-thirds vote. On the first ballot (interminable nominating and seconding speeches had not yet come into fashion) Van Buren scored 146, Cass 83, while there were scattered votes for Calhoun, Johnson, Stewart, Buchanan, and Senator Levi Woodbury of New Hampshire. That was Van Buren's high point. Thereafter he slipped, until on the seventh ballot his vote was in the 90's, while Lewis Cass's vote was a little above 100. Yet it was obvious, at adjournment, that neither man could win. A compromise candidate must be found.

Many of the delegates did not go to bed at all that night, and among these was George Bancroft the historian, a member of the Massachusetts delegation, who, with other members of that delegation, had an interesting confabulation with the New Yorkers. If they could not get Van Buren the New Yorkers wanted another man from their state, Governor Silas Wright, a proven administrator. Wright, however, might refuse to accept the nomination out of loyalty to his dear friend Martin Van Buren; and he was not there to ask.

They settled at last—it was broad daylight by that time —on James Knox Polk, a man who had served two terms as Speaker of the House of Representatives and one term as Governor of Tennessee, though he had failed to get the governorship on two subsequent occasions; a man, in short, whom very few outside of his home state had ever heard of, and who had been mentioned, at most, as a possible *vice* presidential candidate in case the presidential nomination itself went to a Northerner or an Easterner, like Van Buren. The New Yorkers agreed.

Next morning, on the eighth ballot, the leaders remained about the same, deadlocked, 104 for Van Buren, 114 for Cass, but 44 votes had been cast for James K. Polk.

That started the landslide. The tenth ballot was unanimous for Polk, though men everywhere were still asking who in hell *he* was.

Well, he was a dour, unpleasant, smallish man of Scots ancestry, a prodigiously stubborn man who had very little imagination and no sense of humor at all. He was a fighter. He was for annexation, no matter what the cost.[15]

He was the first "dark horse" in American political history.[16]

The First Dark Horse 67

Wednesday what remained of the delegates voted by a large majority for Silas Wright as Vice President, but Wright, indignant at what he called the "insult" the convention had put upon New York when it failed to nominate Martin Van Buren, refused. His refusal was sent to Baltimore by the recently invented electric telegraph, the first time it had been used for this purpose.

Thursday, after this refusal had been verified by means of a written message carried by a horseman—for some of the delegates were disinclined to trust that newfangled electric device—a weary convention nominated George M. Dallas of Pennsylvania for Vice President (an Easterner obviously was called for, to balance the ticket) and adopted a platform.

The platform was similar to that adopted in 1840, but it contained an additional plank calling for "the reoccupation of Oregon and the reannexation of Texas, at the earliest practicable period."

Thus the issue went to the voters.

The campaign was exceptionally dirty. All sorts of men called Henry Clay all sorts of things—from a safe distance—and as for Polk, the Whigs gleefully printed what purported to be a travelogue by one Roorbach, in which this mysterious Englishman reported having seen, in Tennessee, a whole gang of Negro slaves with the initials "J. K. P." branded on their foreheads, thus giving the American language a new word—"Roorbach."

The vote was very close. The Democrats carried Louisiana by only 700, and Polk lost his own state of Tennessee by 113. New York was the crucial state. Clay lost it by barely 5,000, though the Liberty Party candidates had polled 15,-812 there, many of which, probably most of which, almost certainly would have gone to the Whig ticket had the abolitionists not stood for office. Polk got 170 electors to Clay's 105, but the popular vote was closer than that: 1,337,243 for Polk, 1,299,062 for Clay.[17]

The country was committed.

CHAPTER

9

The Hot Potato

GIVEN THE DIFFERENCES in temperament, in language, in background, the wonder is that these two proud nations, Mexico and the United States, had lived together on the same continent for as long as they did.

Mexican diplomats were a voluble lot and not infrequently contradicted one another or changed verbiage in mid-sentence; but they sang in unison, their voices exquisitely harmonizing, when they expressed dispraise of the idea that Texas might be annexed to the United States of America. Annexation, they said—and they said it many times, iterating and reiterating it, sometimes in a loud voice, again softly, but always emphatically—annexation meant war.

Annexation was the hot potato of American politics. It was passed around, hurriedly.

After San Jacinto the Texans, almost to a man, wished to be taken into the American Union, and made a formal request to this effect. They were free, but how long could they stay free? San Jacinto had been a miracle, and it was well not to count upon miracles, which did not often happen. The Republic of Mexico had a population of about

8,000,000; the Republic of Texas had a population of about 50,000. Ergo: Texas could not go it alone. It was as simple as that.

Yet there was more. The Texans were virtually all Americans, most of them recently out. Religion, background, habits, outlook, language, all pointed to a merger. When the restless Southerner scribbled "Gone to Texas" in chalk on his house, or simply "G.T.T.," he did not think of himself as leaving his own country, only as going to another part of that country. Nothing could have been more natural. The leaders might sometimes have hesitated, enjoying, as they did, this heady new power; but in the minds of the rank and file there was never any question about where they belonged. If Uncle Sam (the name was new, and the older Brother Jonathan still was widely used) was to be no more than a cold neighbor, why then, what would happen to the Texans when the greasers came back in force?

There was much talk among the early settlers, who just at first took annexation for granted, of splitting Texas into two, three, or even four separate parts, each of which, it was assumed, in time would become a state entitled to its own two United States senators. This did not appeal to the New Englanders, who thought that the South already was too strong in the Senate, and who did not wish to sit by and watch the land become ineradicably committed to slave laws. John Quincy Adams and twelve other members of the House of Representatives were so alarmed that they issued a circular decrying "the undue ascendancy of the slaveholding power" and declaring that "this nefarious project" of annexing Texas could easily end in the dissolution of the Union. It was shrill, this manifesto; but that it influenced many votes can be doubted. But Adams, a hard hitter, could never be ignored.

It is notable that annexationists always referred to *re*-annexation, just as they referred to the occupation of the vast Oregon Territory, concerning which the United States was having angry words with Great Britain, as *re*-occupation. The argument in each case was the same. Oregon [18] had been explored, at least along its sea edges, by the British, but it had been actually occupied by Americans in the fur trade, and hence it was, in American eyes, American. It could be *re*-occupied as far north as the southernmost Russian claims, which was the line of latitude 54′ 40″, and indeed the cry "Fifty-four forty or fight!" was loud in the land. By the same token the *re*-annexationists contended that the territory of Texas as far south as the Rio Grande had properly been a part of the Louisiana Purchase. If we annexed Texas, they insisted, we would not be taking something that didn't belong to us: we would only be taking back something that had been ours all along. That we had forsworn our claim to the land west of the Sabine when we bought the Floridas from Spain made no difference to these zealots. We were dealing with Mexico now, they said, not with Spain. The Florida Purchase treaty no longer had any standing.

The Democrats in their party platform of 1844 cunningly linked those *re*'s, asserting that we should seize Oregon and Texas alike, presumably simultaneously. In this way they hoped to get Northerners and Southerners working together.

On the other hand, such an action might result in war with Mexico and Great Britain at the same time, which would be disconcerting.

Recognition of Texas as an independent republic was easy enough. That was done March 31, 1837, by the United States, and other powers soon followed suit.

Annexation would be a thornier matter. Jackson had still been President then, and he was personally in favor of the annexation of Texas, but as the end of his second term approached, he did not wish to embarrass his successor, Van Buren, with a *fait accompli* that might kick back. Prompt

annexation, he had feared, would make it look to Mexico—
and indeed to the whole world—that the United States really
had been behind those bands of armed men who infiltrated
the frontier, and that the whole thing was, as Mexico had
always claimed, a gigantic swindle. So Jackson held his
hand.

Van Buren had felt the same way about it. During his
four years as President there were sporadic annexation
moves, but for the most part the Fox of Kinderhook managed to evade the issue.

Whether William Henry Harrison had any opinions on
the subject will never be known, for his sponsor and secretary of state, Daniel Webster, stood in his stead as a sort of
spokesman, telling him what to say, if anything, in public;
and Webster was opposed to annexation. When Harrison
died so soon after his inauguration and John ("Tyler and
Texas!") Tyler succeeded him, it might have been assumed
that the matter would come up again. But Webster stayed
on at state, the only member of the cabinet who did not
quit at Harrison's death, and we may believe that the new
President was somewhat afraid of him, for Webster could
in all truth be a formidable foe. Webster was enwrapped in
his negotiations with the British foreign office, striving to
straighten out the Canadian border dispute, both in Maine
and in the Oregon Territory; he had no time for Texas.
Besides, Texas, tired of waiting at the church door all togged
out in bridal veil and orange blossoms, had opened talks
with Mexico on the possibility of an armistice. Mexico was
prepared to grant almost anything except independence,
and Texas would consider nothing less, so the talks were
unproductive, but they lasted a little over two years and in
that time of course it would hardly do to push annexation,
a touchy topic with the Mexicans.

When at last the two republics to the south had agreed
once more to disagree, and Daniel Webster had removed

his mighty presence from the Department of State, President Tyler, doubtless whooshing with relief, appointed a more sympathetic secretary, a fellow Southerner, a friend, Abel P. Upshur, who was an annexationist, and who immediately went into session with the Texas commissioners in Washington for the purpose of framing a treaty. The nature of the talks was secret; but they were believed to have been coming along very nicely when a new naval gun Upshur was examining (he had formerly been Secretary of the Navy) went off accidentally, killing him and sundry others; and the whole business had to be begun again.

It must have been with some trepidation that President Tyler appointed to the vacant post the redoubtable John Calhoun, temporarily out of the Senate; for though the South Carolinian was a man of great force and character, and fervently in favor of annexation, he had a tendency to hog the center of the stage, taking all the credit to himself. Tyler at this time was still hoping to put annexation through Congress, or at least an annexation treaty through the Senate, before the election of 1844. That could make him the hero of the hour; and since the Whig and Democratic frontrunners, Clay and Van Buren, might offset one another, each being opposed to annexation, Tyler might slip back into the White House. The trouble was, Calhoun had exactly the same idea.

It was Calhoun who developed the beware-of-England technique, which did more than anything else to popularize annexation. Both France and Great Britain had extensive holdings in Mexico, and both in consequence could be expected to take an interest in the status of Texas, which presently formed a buffer state. If either of those powers were to gain control of Texas, as a result of no matter what behind-the-scenes arrangement, the United States could expect a great upsurge of smuggling along a border hard to patrol. The Northerners and Easterners, most of them Whigs, who had worked so long and hard for a high tariff, would then be ruined. On the other hand, if slavery was abolished in Texas through the machinations of Great Britain, which recently had freed all the slaves in its own empire, then Texas would constitute a built-in escape hatch. A slave who fled to Canada, though he might be helped by any number of so-called underground railroad organizations those damn Yankees had organized, must pass through many states, in any one of which he might be arrested, and by federal law he must then be returned to his owner. A slave who escaped to a Texas controlled by those damn English abolitionists could thereupon thumb his nose at any pursuers. The very thought made John Calhoun boil. He said that such a state of affairs could only end in a servile uprising and race war.

Calhoun's was a strong but not a flexible mind, and when he believed anything he believed it at the top of his voice.

France did not go unsuspected, but it was at England that most public fingers were pointed. Americans were ready to believe almost anything about the perfidious English, and when a rumor went the rounds that Great Britain had offered Texas an enormous loan on condition that she abolish slavery they swallowed it by the hundreds of thousands, though there was not a scintilla of evidence that Britain had done any such thing, either officially or "out of doors."

Even so, Tyler and Calhoun could not cram their annexation treaty through the Senate before the election. The Senators wanted to know first which way that cat would jump when it was let out of the bag. Seven days after the 1844 Democratic convention in Baltimore they turned down the treaty, thirty-six to fifteen.

Nobody could deny, however, that the election itself might be taken as a pro-annexation mandate. Polk had won; and that was that.

He lost no time. As soon as he got into the White House he started to push annexation through both houses of Congress in the form of a joint resolution rather than in the form of a treaty, the trick Tyler had tried. It was close, but it won. Texas at long last would be invited to join the Union.

The Mexican ambassador demanded his passports.

CHAPTER

10

Dark Doings

SECRETARIES OF STATE during the period of prewar strain had been a notably strong lot—Clay, Webster, Upshur, Calhoun, and now, under Polk, James Buchanan. With ambassadors and chargés d'affaires it was not so. The first to be sent to the newly recognized Mexican Republic, Joel Roberts Poinsett, an amateur botanist, though he was asked to leave because of his meddling Masonic activities, did bring back the flashy, red, long-petaled flower that was named after him, *Poinsettia pulcherrima*. The others, Anthony Butler,[19] Powhatan Ellis, Waddy Thompson, Wilson Shannon, brought back only hard feelings.

It was hoped that John Slidell of New Orleans would do better.

The situation in Mexico, never static, was in a state of especial turbulence just at this time, was indeed near anarchy. Santa Anna, that Yo-Yo, was in one of his downs. His wife, a long-suffering woman too shy to appear in public but beloved by the populace all the same, had recently died, and in indecent haste, a matter of mere weeks, the man had married a seventeen-year-old, a strident, small harridan who was to lead him around by the nose. This the people could not forgive. Santa Anna's morals always had been low, but the people could overlook those many mistresses, for weren't generals usually like that? An immediate remarriage was different. So Santa Anna, for this and other reasons, was exiled, though he did succeed in retaining all of his estates. Just to show how they felt about the business, members of a mob in Mexico City smashed open the ornate mausoleum in which the General's severed leg had lain so long in state; and they hacked the relic, and spat upon it, and tossed it into the public dump.

The exile was not onerous. He spent it in Havana, to which he had taken what was probably the world's biggest stable of fighting cocks.

José Joaquín Herrera, who had succeeded Santa Anna as President, was married to a *norteamericano* woman, and was not, as so many Mexican *politicos* were, a Yanqui baiter. Behind Herrera—perhaps a trifle too close behind—was General Mariano Paredes y Arrillaga, who was at the head of the army, just then in a state of near-mutiny because there wasn't any money.

James K. Polk, in Washington, was a man who listened a lot without opening his own mouth, and at any given time it was difficult to guess what he was thinking. He believed that Herrera, properly approached, might be induced to receive and talk with an American ambassador. The United States still maintained consuls in Mexico City and Vera Cruz, but its minister at Mexico City had of course been recalled when the Mexican ambassador in Washington had gone home in a huff.

Polk sent to Mexico one W. S. Parrott, a dentist who could speak Spanish, as a personal representative with no official status, assigned to sound out Herrera. This Parrott did, and he returned to report that Herrera would be willing to receive an American minister. Or maybe he said "commissioner" instead. The point was to be much discussed. Certainly President Polk thought of the man appointed,

John Slidell, as a minister, and repeatedly referred to him as such.[20]

Slidell actually was authorized to act as an envoy extraordinary and minister plenipotentiary, and equipped with papers to this effect, though the United States Senate was not even notified, for the mission was to be a secret one. Slidell departed November 10, 1845.

Much thought had gone into the framing of Slidell's instructions. President Polk was no longer concerned with the annexation of Texas; that was a thing done. Texas alone would not satisfy this expansionist. He wanted all of New Mexico as well, and all of upper California, *alta* California. The United States would get that land sooner or later anyway, he reasoned, and the deed might best be done when the time was right, as he believed it was now. Slidell, a New York lawyer, a Columbia graduate, who had settled in New Orleans and married into one of the most aristocratic of Creole families, and who could speak both Spanish and French, was told to treat for these territories, offering either cash or a lifting of American claims.

France and Great Britain were not the only powers who had filed huge claims against the rampageous Mexican government. United States citizens demanded millions in reparations; and their case had been dragging for years before Mexico at last agreed to submit it, or part of it, to an arbitration board consisting of three Mexicans, three Americans, and an umpire appointed by the King of Prussia. This was done, and after a while the board found about 30 percent of the claims valid and had ordered payment by Mexico. Mexico had no money and asked if the payments could not be spread over twenty years, and to this the United States had agreed. Three annual payments had been made, and then there were no more, nor was there any explanation or apology. This had nothing to do with the annexation of Texas, but it was still a sore point between the two nations.

John Quincy Adams, when President, had offered Mexico $1,000,000 for Texas. President Jackson had offered $5,000,000. Both of these offers had been spurned. Now Texas had been annexed without any purchase price (though the republic was about $10,000,000 in debt, which debt the Federal government took over) and James K. Polk was interested in getting all the rest of the Mexican territory as far west as the Pacific.

He made no bones about this. He thought that he could get it for something between $15,000,000 and $20,000,000, but he was willing to go as high as $40,000,000,[21] and he so instructed John Slidell.

The Secretary of State, Buchanan, was opposed to this. He was engaged in negotiations with Great Britain on the matter of Oregon, and he was afraid that the situation might lead to war; but he was overruled.

Slidell never met Herrera, who threw up his hands in despair when he learned that the visitor had been accredited as a minister rather than as a mere commissioner. To receive a minister would be the equivalent of endorsing the annexation of Texas, which would never do. Herrera, in those circumstances, would not last two hours in the President's seat, already a wobbly piece of furniture. Paredes, as he well knew, was breathing against the back of his neck; and Paredes was a vehement hater of the neighbors to the north.

Slidell did not hurry home but retired quietly to Jalapa, where he would wait and see, for he believed that there would be a change of Presidents soon.

He was right. Herrera held out only a few more weeks, and was succeeded by Paredes, who acted as President ad interim. However, this did Slidell no good, for Paredes would be even less willing to receive him; and at last he went back to the States.

For nine years, under whatever President, Mexico had made no serious, sustained effort to recover Texas. There had been bluster in plenty, and there had been across-the-border raids for hostages, but there had not been any large-scale military movement. In that time not only the United States but most of the European mercantile nations had recognized Texas as an independent republic; yet Mexico still insisted that Texas was an integral part of Mexico and that, therefore, annexation on the part of the United States was a *casus belli*. Nobody in Mexican public life really believed that the strayed state was recoverable, but nobody in Mexican public life dared to admit this openly, such was the public's pride.

Grimly President Polk set about making preparations for conflict. Commodore John D. Sloat, in charge of the Pacific fleet, was instructed to be prepared to seize San Francisco Bay and other desirable spots as soon as he heard for sure that war existed. Commodore David Conner, in charge of the Atlantic fleet, was instructed to concentrate his vessels along the Gulf coast of Mexico and be prepared at a moment's notice to establish a blockade. A special message was sent to the United States consul at Monterey, California, one Thomas O. Larkin (the same man who had disillusioned Thomas Ap Catesby Jones), urging him to assure such residents of the district as might be interested that the United States would welcome California into the Union any time she really cared to come. This last was not as ambitious a project as it might seem. The Californias, upper and lower, had for long chafed under the distant but harsh hand of Mexico City, and upper California had recently staged something akin to a revolution of its own, so that it was currently a semi-independent state and doubtless contained many large landowners who, though themselves Mexican, would welcome the security of *norteamericano* rule.

President Polk did nothing to increase the size of the United States Army, a mere seven thousand men, or somewhat less than a third of the number Mexico habitually kept under arms, but he did cause General Zachary Taylor, in charge of the army in the southwest, to call in certain far-flung frontier units and to stand ready near the Texas-Louisiana line.

War had not been declared, but it might almost as well have been.

CHAPTER

11

Jacta Est Alea

FEBRUARY 13 OF THE YEAR 1846 a rather sinister figure came calling at the White House. This was Colonel A. J. Atocha, a Spaniard by birth, an American by naturalization, and a friend of Antonio Lopez de Santa Anna, whom he had visited at Havana the previous month. President Polk, though he had a full waiting room, gave Colonel Atocha a whole hour, it being understood that the talk would be confidential.

Atocha said that Santa Anna, wooden leg and all—"the immortal three-quarters" he was sometimes called—was still very much of a vital force in Mexican politics. The captain general of Cuba, Don Leopoldo O'Donell, had made much of the distinguished visitor, though Santa Anna had discreetly declined an invitation to an Independence Day dinner at the American consulate, which would have hurt him among the anti-Yanqui men at home. Every time a vessel arrived from Mexico, Atocha said, Santa Anna received hundreds of letters pledging support. He was in close touch with the political tangle in Mexico City, and had approved, if he had not actually engineered the taking-over by Paredes, the ousting of Herrera. He could himself take over from Paredes any time he felt like it, this crony said, *if* the United

States Navy would permit him to make that trip *and* if the United States Treasury would advance him enough money to pay the discontented Mexican army. That was the big problem, avowed Atocha—money. How much? Oh, about thirty million dollars.

President Polk listened carefully, but made no comment. That night he recorded the interview in his diary, and the next morning he reported it to a meeting of the cabinet. Secretary Buchanan didn't think that anything definite should be done about the man in Cuba until the business of Oregon had been straightened out and the danger of war in *that* quarter eliminated. The others, however, were interested. The President confessed that he did not trust Atocha personally—he didn't like the man's looks—but thought that there might be something in what he said.

Two days after this cabinet meeting Colonel Atocha came to the White House again, twice, once in the morning, again in the afternoon, and was closeted with the President for a long time on each visit.

A show of strength was what he urged; an army on the border, a fleet off the coast. The visitor himself had filed a large claim against the Mexican government, and of course he hoped to see his friend Santa Anna get back into the Presidency, so that this claim might be paid; but even the great Santa Anna himself could not venture to pay any claims of the despised Yanquis unless and until he had a gun pointed at his head. What, uh, what was the matter with thirty million dollars?

No official action was taken, but a thought had been opened, a possible course indicated.

Zachary Taylor was anything but the very model of a modern major general. He was thickset, with short legs but a long body, clumsy of movement. He was literate, but his education had been limited, and elegance was something he did not know about. He had a seamed, weatherbeaten face, and looked, as he talked, like a farmer. The men liked him, and trusted him. "Old Zack" they sometimes called him, or sometimes it was "Old Rough-and-Ready." Rough he assuredly was. He had a passion for sloppy clothes, a highly unmilitary distaste for trimness. He was sometimes called a scarecrow, but there were those who contended that this epithet flattered him. He used to wear a dirty, badly pressed handkerchief around his neck, and he often forgot to fasten on the insignia of his rank. He did not even sit a horse as a soldier should, but sprawled in the saddle, often with both legs on the same side, like a woman, or with one foot or one knee propped against the pommel.

That horse, parenthetically, was called "Old Whitey." The adjective "old," applied affectionately with nicknames, was exceedingly popular at the time—Old Kinderhook, Old Hickory, and so forth—but Old Rough-and-Ready really was old for a general, sixty, almost sixty-one, at the time he was ordered from Baton Rouge into Texas to be a threatening force near the border, a move that was almost sure to bring about a war. Moreover, he was in poor health, and feeling his years, and he often complained. He was subject to bilious attacks.

Corpus Christi, a hovel of about twenty shacks, was the farthest west as it was the farthest south of the state occupied by Texans in the fall of 1845 when Taylor and his men reached there by boat from New Orleans. They proceeded to set up a camp along the east bank of the Nueces. These men numbered almost four thousand, more than half of the United States Army, the greatest military assemblage since the War of 1812. They were all regulars, and about a third of them were not American but Irish, German, French, Polish, English. They were formed into one regiment of dragoons, five regiments of infantry, and four batteries of field artillery.

The officers were delighted. It was the first time that they had been given a chance to drill by regiments and brigades instead of just by companies.

Across the river was a stretch of land from 100 to 150 miles wide, largely wilderness, entirely uninhabited, stretching to the Rio Grande, or Rio Bravo as it was often called. This was land of no strategic value but important because it was disputed. Texas had claimed it before the Texan revolt, and still claimed it, which meant that the United States also claimed it; but Mexico insisted that it was a part of the province of Tamaulipas and never had belonged to Texas anyway.

Corpus Christi boomed. "Grocers"—a euphemism for grog-shop proprietors—flourished. Sutlers yammered of their wares. Washwomen charged the soldiers fifty cents a month to do their laundry. Privates were paid only seven dollars a month—"seven-dollar targets" they liked to call themselves —but a dollar went a long way in country like that.

There were horse races almost every day. The men built their own theatre, seating eight hundred, and painted their own scenery, and put on their own shows. Some of these shows were pretentious, despite the fact that in the absence of women men had to play the female parts; when they staged *Othello*, for instance, the Desdemona was a somewhat chunky young lieutenant fresh out of West Point named U. S. Grant.

It was in January that orders came from Washington to proceed to the Rio Grande. In Mexican eyes the entrance into Texas by a Federal force was in itself an act of war, but to penetrate the disputed territory between the Nueces and the Rio Grande would be doubly so. It began to look as if Washington *wanted* a fight.[22] But—Taylor had his orders, and he obeyed them.

He took his time. He wished to have the land between the rivers well scouted before he ventured upon it, and he arranged to have his sick—there was a great deal of malaria —taken to the more southern encampment by sea, under the protection of United States Navy vessels. It was March before he started to march, and it was nearing April when his column reached the Arroyo Colorado, only a few miles from the Rio Grande.

This was a considerable body of salt water, where trouble could be expected. Mexicans lay on the other side, and a message to General Taylor stated—bombastically, as was the custom—that if the Yanquis attempted to cross the Arroyo the Mexicans would resist to the last drop of their blood.

There was a great deal of noise over there—shouted orders, the flapping of flags, roll of drums, blast of bugles— but there were no shots.

Old Rough-and-Ready went ahead with his preparations to cross, and cross he did, unopposed. The Mexicans had melted away. They proved in fact to have been a much smaller force than they had pretended to be, having been skillfully scattered, and no doubt their commander did not want to take upon himself the responsibility of having started a war.

The Americans established a base of supplies at Point Isabel, on the Gulf about ten miles from their camp on the Rio Grande just opposite the town of Matamoros, which was the headquarters of Mejía, the Mexican general. A more explosive location would have been hard to find.

Mejía soon was replaced by General Pedro de Ampudia, who brought with him two thousand reinforcements. Ampudia solemnly warned Taylor to break camp and start back for the Nueces within twenty-four hours or face the consequences. To this Taylor replied that he reckoned he'd stay where he was. The Americans started to build a fort there. They called it Fort Texas.

Outwardly everything was calm. There was still some malaria, and there was a great deal of desertion on the part of the Americans, especially the Irishmen, for the stream was narrow and shallow and the Mexicans sent out all sorts of printed enticements, offering even a private 320 acres. But there was no shooting. The fishing was excellent, the hunting too. A colonel, out for a little hunting of his own, mysteriously got himself killed on the east bank; but this could have been the work of some stray bandits. At night the men would line up along the banks of the river, on each side, and sing, while the bands played. The Mexican bands were by far the better.

Ampudia was replaced by General Mariano Arista, a tall, freckle-faced, red-whiskered man who as an exile had spent some years in Cincinnati and could speak English, which fact somehow made him seem more human. It was Arista, however, who first crossed the river. He sent 1,600 cavalry over.

Hearing of this, that same night, General Taylor sent off a scouting party of sixty-three dragoons under Captain Seth Thornton. These men, the following day, were surrounded in a ranch house north of Fort Texas. Eleven of them were killed, and most of the rest were either wounded or taken prisoner. Only a few escaped to tell the tale.

Now Old Rough-and-Ready went into action. It was April 26, 1846, and he sent a searing letter to the President in Washington, pointing out that this had been a regular action, not merely a bit of disorder: it had been a spilling of American blood on American soil.

James K. Polk caught at that phrase about American blood when he got the letter just after he came home from church May 10 (it was a Sunday). He sat down and wrote a message to Congress asking for war. He sent this off the next morning, to both houses. The Representatives passed it promptly, 173 to 14. The Senate took another day to talk, and passed the measure, with minor changes, Tuesday, May 12. The House concurred in the changes, and President Polk signed the bill on Wednesday, May 13.

The thing was done. This was war.

CHAPTER

12

Two Romps

ONE THING AT LEAST was certain: This would be no David-and-Goliath encounter. In extent of territory the two republics were about equal, but the United States had more than twice the population of Mexico, the United States had a navy while Mexico had none, and the United States was both wealthy and highly industrialized whereas Mexico was bankrupt and without industry; moreover, it should be remembered that Mexico had a proud military tradition, while the United States seemed to be ashamed of its army and even as the war clouds gathered Congress was considering a suggestion that the United States Military Academy at West Point be abandoned as useless.[23] Neither side was well organized for the purpose of waging war,[24] though the Mexicans, what with all their revolutions, had much more experience on the field of battle. It should be remembered too that Mexico had a standing army of more than thirty thousand, four times the size of the United States Army.

The Mexican leaders were cocky. They were unanimous in the belief that they would not have to fight the whole of the neighbor to the north anyway, only the southern and perhaps western portions of it, for New England, they were sure, and probably New York and Pennsylvania as well, would drop out of the Union as soon as hostilities began. Moreover, they believed that they would not be fighting alone, that Great Britain would soon get into the thing, either as a clandestine ally of Mexico or else openly as a nation at war with the United States. The Oregon problem was far from being settled: it remained a porcupine with every quill quivering. Cries of "Fifty-four forty or fight!" still rang in the Washington air, and Buchanan, the worrying type, worried.

There was no war party in Washington, nothing to match the enthusiasm that prevailed in Mexico City. There were no "hawks," as there had been just before the outbreak of the War of 1812. Congress, on the contrary, seemed to be made up entirely of men who sought peace—or said that they did, even the Southerners.

All of this was changed by the news from Texas. Abruptly, the nation fumed. The war act passed by both houses of Congress appropriated $10,000,000 for the conduct of the war and authorized the President to accept volunteers for one-year terms or for the duration up to the number of 50,000. Recruits began to pour in. This was no regional matter; and there were no further mutterings about secession.

Meanwhile, in Texas, Zachary Taylor had made it final.

Those cavalrymen who had rounded up Seth Thornton's command were to have been the northern part of what General Arista planned to be a pincerlike movement on the east bank of the Rio Grande. They had crossed well upriver from Fort Texas and Matamoros. Soon afterward the main Mexican body crossed the river about ten miles *below* Fort Texas, the plan being to join the others just east of Fort Texas on the road to Point Isabel, thus getting between Taylor and his base of supplies.

Arista was slow getting started, perhaps because he and the man he had relieved and who was now his second-in-command, General Ampudia, simply could not get along. Whatever the reason, he was not across the river in force until May 3, and by that time Taylor was already at Point Isabel.

Fort Texas was a triangular open-topped structure that sat on a point of land jutting out into the river. Two of its sides were thus protected by water. It was considered very strong. Old Rough-and-Ready left one regiment of infantry and two companies of artillery there, besides the sick, perhaps five hundred men altogether, in charge of Major Jacob Brown and two subalterns, Captain Loud and Lieutenant Bragg.[25] All the rest of the army he took to Point Isabel, leaving the afternoon of May 1 and reaching the base the next day, without having seen anything of the enemy. The distance was about twenty-five miles.

The water off Point Isabel, like the water at most points along that coast, was exceedingly shallow. Supplies had to be lightered from vessels anchored two miles out, which took time. There had now been amassed a considerable store, and it was this that Taylor had come to fetch, though while he was at it he also strengthened the defenses of the place. That he took with him such a strong force suggests that he expected Ampudia to try to intercept him on his return. He was to be even stronger when he started to go back, having taken from the garrison men who were replaced by a small company of volunteers arriving from New Orleans at just this time and also by about five hundred Marines and bluejackets lent him by Captain Gregory of the standing-by U.S.S. *Raritan*.

He stayed five days at Point Isabel, and on the second day, May 3, he heard cannon fire from the direction of the Rio Grande, from which he adduced that Fort Texas was being bombarded from Matamoros; but he did not worry about this.

The men in the fort did not worry much about it either.

Now and then a ball would come in, but the men soon learned to walk around the walls rather than across the center, and few of them were hit.

One of the unlucky ones, however, was the commanding officer, Major Brown, whose leg was smashed by stone chips flying from the place where a cannonball had ricochetted. They had to amputate the leg. Brown lay on his cot for two days, in great pain but cheerful, directing the defense of the fort; and then he died. They renamed the place Fort Brown.[26]

When Taylor pulled out of Point Isabel he may have had almost 2,500 in his command. These included dragoons, infantry, and artillerymen, for the force contained two batteries of field guns besides two enormous eighteen-pounders, but the most conspicuous part of his column consisted of some three hundred just-made wagons filled with ammunition and food supplies, and pulled, most of them, by oxen. It was the supply train that was the real purpose of this march.

Arista was waiting for him with well over twice as many men.

They made contact Friday, May 8, at a place called Palo Alto.

Arista had picked his ground well. Before him was open prairie, while his right rested on a small hill, his left on a swampy wood. Despite his superiority in numbers he showed no inclination to advance but simply stood his ground.

Taylor ordered an attack.

This was a little after two o'clock in the afternoon.

At first, though a few skirmishing flank parties did scrape, it was largely an artillery duel. The American guns, superbly handled, did great damage, cutting down Mexicans in swathes. *They*, the Mexicans, pleaded to be allowed to attack or else be withdrawn out of the range of those terrible cannons; but Arista, who did not want to give up the advantage of his position, kept them where they were; and their morale wobbled.

The Mexican guns must have been badly handled or else they were using a poor grade of powder, for most of them fired too low, the balls bouncing and skipping through the prairie grass, so that the Americans could see them coming and spring out of the way.

The grass caught fire, nobody knew how, and the smoke was so thick on that windless day that it was necessary to call off the battle for an hour or more.

Under cover of this smoke both sides regrouped, each, as it happened, being intent upon smashing the other's left. When the smoke lifted the tearful men charged, but the fight was inconclusive. Neither line broke. The Mexicans held the field, but their losses had been much heavier than the American losses and they were in a badly demoralized condition. In the darkness Arista withdrew them to a couple of deep dry ravines, formerly riverbeds, called the Resaca de Guerrero and the Resaca de la Palma. These positions were screened by chaparral so thick—a jungle of cactus and briar—that the dreaded American fieldpieces would be useless.

Taylor, who had been moving his men since a little after dawn, stopped before Resaca de la Palma, and studied the situation. There was one natural alley through which he could use his cannons: it led to the Mexican right. He was about to open the attack when some of his senior officers asked for a council of war, to which he agreed. It was the consensus that the position was too strong to be stormed, and that if the Americans, who were well supplied with food, simply sat before it, the Mexicans sooner or later would have to pull out toward the Rio Grande, where the

THE DRAGOONS CHARGED, WITH SABERS FLASHING

ground was flat and there was no chaparral. Taylor heard them out, and then cast his own vote—the only one that counted—against them; he ordered an advance.

The dragoons went in first, and they did a slam-bang job of it, capturing several guns and one general.[27] When they had returned, the artillery opened up. Meanwhile the infantry was wriggling its painful way through the chaparral in the center and on the left, and this same tangle that so limited the fieldpieces served as cover for the foot soldiers, who because of it were able to spring upon the enemy unexpectedly. The fighting that followed was savage, hand-to-hand. Men lost their officers, officers their men, and everything was mixed up.

Arista, in his pavilion, heard the shooting, but he assumed that it was a mere feeling-out, for he was sure that his position was impregnable. By the time he learned the truth and ran outside, it was too late. The Mexicans everywhere were in a rout. They did not stop running until they got back to the Rio Grande.

If Palo Alto had been an artilleryman's victory, Resaca de la Palma was an infantryman's. The Mexicans' cannon fire had been low in the one fight, their musket fire much too high in the other. Both sides carried old-fashioned flint-and-steel muskets, percussion caps still being thought too undependable for battle. The Americans had a gun made at Springfield that was probably as good a smoothbore weapon as there was in the world. The Mexicans carried Tower muskets, the famous Brown Bess, which the British army had retired a few years ago in favor of the newfangled rifle. These were good guns, durable, dependable, easy to reload, but they had no front sight, for they were not meant to be deliberately aimed at anything but only to be pointed in the general direction of the enemy and fired on command. These guns packed a heavy kick, which the Mexicans did not like. Also, if there was any sort of breeze against the muzzle they had a tendency to flare back at the touch hole, which could do nasty things to the shooter's face. The British soldiers had been trained to turn their heads aside in these circumstances, but the Mexicans did not like to take even that small risk of having their eyebrows scorched off, and habitually—though it was against regulations—they fired from the hip. This meant that they fired too high. At least nineteen out of every twenty bullets shot at the oncoming Americans at Resaca de la Palma whizzed off into the air above their heads.

The Americans did not pursue. For one thing, it was getting dark. For another, they were tired; though it had been a short fight it had been furious. Then too, the loot had to be examined. And finally, neither Zachary Taylor nor anyone else in his army had the slightest idea of the extent of the Mexican panic, which was complete.

The loot included all the Mexican cannons, all the supplies, six hundred mules and pack saddles, hundreds of thrown-away Tower muskets, and a very large number of bodies, for the Mexican casualties numbered more than eight hundred, compared with a little over a hundred for the Americans. The Americans had not nabbed Arista himself—the general the dragoons did get was named Vega—but they had his tremendous, truly princely tent, a palace, with elaborate heavy furniture, with all the general's spare swords, medals, and uniforms, and his entire body of correspondence. In that correspondence they were delighted to find a letter from President Paredes ordering General Arista, after he had smashed the Yanqui army, to send Zachary Taylor a prisoner to Mexico City.

CHAPTER

13

A Tough Nut to Crack

WE DID NOT GET fifty-four forty, nor did we fight. The long-standing dispute about Oregon was settled quietly, a compromise on the 49th parallel of latitude, in June of that momentous year 1846. Buchanan could breathe again.

It was as well that Congress had limited enlistments to 50,000. State after state almost immediately oversupplied its quota and had to turn applicants away. Mexico had always been in the popular imagination a place of glitter and glamour, with its silver mines, its volcanos, its desert, and its señoritas; "the halls of Montezuma" was a phrase on everyone's tongue; and the youth of the land couldn't get to the recruiting offices fast enough.

Brigadier Stephen W. Kearny, fifty-two years old, a small man with gray hair and large pale eyes, a quiet man, no blusterer, was among the first to receive marching orders, and he had no difficulty raising 1,500 frontiersmen in the vicinity of Fort Leavenworth. This was known as the Army of the West, and with it he set a course for Santa Fe.

The vast province of New Mexico, like that of California, was semi-independent, a law unto itself. These had not been formally disowned by the Federal government, but they were too far away to be bothered with when the *politicos* had so much to trouble them at home, so that they were allowed to bumble along in their own fashion.

New Mexico offered no opposition to the fast-approaching Kearny. At the village of Las Vegas he was met by a messenger under a white flag, who delivered an ultimatum from the fat governor, Armijo. The Yanquis must turn around promptly and march back to where they came from or he would squash them without mercy. Kearny, a slab-sided man with seamed cheeks, paid no attention to this threat but marched on. He took Santa Fe—the men called it a "mud town"—August 18. He raised the Stars and Stripes, issued a proclamation absolving all citizens of their obligations to Mexico, declared himself governor, and began to govern. Armijo had already decamped for the capital.

It was a model invasion. Kearny had led 1,500 men more than 1,000 miles through country strange to all of them, a country that offered many natural defenses—in six weeks. He had seized this country and its 80,000 inhabitants without firing a shot.

He wasted no time. He dispatched a force under Colonel Alexander W. Doniphan, a Missouri lawyer, to march through Chihuahua, a province noted for its hairless dogs, and to join Taylor on the Rio Grande; and then, without even waiting for his expected reinforcements, Kearny persuaded the scout Kit Carson to guide him and three hundred of his men to Los Angeles, a somewhat important place in the southern part of Upper California, where they were to join forces under the command of Commodore Robert F. Stockton, U.S.N., and the erratic, unpredictable Captain John Charles Frémont, U.S.A., in the conquest of California. It was California that James K. Polk had his eye on all the time.

The war, then, was off to a good start, though its opening whirlwind, Zachary Taylor, had grounded to a halt.

General Taylor was not well served by his scouts. He had been encamped at Corpus Christi for six months, but when he got an order to go on to the Rio Grande he had to spend a couple of weeks scouting in that direction before he could venture to start. At Fort Brown after the victories of Palo Alto and Resaca de la Palma any reasonably intelligent observer could have assured him that General Arista was having difficulties with his men, who were deserting in droves. A crossing to Matamoros and a quick attack would undoubtedly have scattered them. Taylor did not seem to know this. He meant to take Matamoros, but first he wanted additional supplies. He made another trip to the base at Point Isabel for this purpose. He was by nature a slow-moving man.

He had a good army, all professionals, and unlike most generals he was not forever clamoring for reinforcements. It was supplies he demanded. So they sent him men.

They *inundated* him with men—militiamen who could only be made to serve for three months, and then six-month recruits. It was not until June 24 that the first regiment of twelve-monthers arrived at his bedraggled camp, and by that time the three-monthers were preparing to depart.

These were raw troops, and their officers, in too many cases, owed their commissions to political pull rather than to any natural aptitude toward leadership. Not that the newcomers paid much attention to their officers anyway! They were a disorderly, complaining lot, bad for discipline, men from whom the regulars kept themselves apart.

Arista had been commanded to hold Matamoros as long as possible, but he knew conditions in the field better than anybody in Mexico City could, and he knew that he wouldn't have any army at all if he did not move to a safer place; so he took it upon himself to evacuate the town, May 17–18. *This* act at least was reported to Taylor, who thereupon crossed the Rio Grande and took possession of

Matamoros, the first Mexican town to fall to the United States forces.

It was not much of a town, and did not, with its surrounding territory, make much of a camping site. The water was bad.[28] The hunting and fishing were excellent, but the problem of firewood was always acute, and a cord, mostly green mesquit, cost $2.50. Later, coal was brought in from Ohio and Pennsylvania, but it was expensive. Ice, too, was brought down in schooners from Boston: the price, $1 a pound. Sutlers, "grocerymen," and whores swarmed around that not admirable camp.[29] There were cases of theft and assault, even a few of rape. The regulars behaved themselves, but some of the volunteers were a disgrace. The sick list was appalling, the death rate high.

None of this appeared to annoy Zachary Taylor, who stayed in his tent most of the time, seldom showing himself to the men. He had something else to think about. The mails were coming fairly steadily now, most of them from New Orleans, and every mail contained many letters begging him to run for President in 1848. It seemed that he already had an organization, a movement. This was a perfectly spontaneous start, for Taylor, though nominally a Whig, was not a member of any political group and almost certainly until this time never had given thought to the possibility of getting high office. He was a plain, simple man, unused to city ways, and the letters upset him, though pleasantly.

Arista had scarcely started to reform his army when he was summoned back to the capital to face a court-martial. He was succeeded by Francisco Mejía, a pockmarked little man who wore blue sunglasses and had a fondness for magniloquent speech. Mejía too knew that any move against the gringos would be vain until he had restored discipline in the ranks, got back many of the deserters, and was reinforced. Meanwhile, he assumed, General Taylor would strike at Monterey.

A Tough Nut to Crack

Monterey, a city of about 10,000 population, garrisoned by about 7,000 of Mejía's men, was the capital of Nuevo Leon. It was not walled, but nature and man alike had contrived to make it a strong position. There were elaborate outworks. The houses themselves were flat-roofed and those roofs were parapeted, so that they could make effective shooting platforms. The streets, being narrow, could easily be barricaded. The cathedral, in the central plaza, was well stocked with ammunition. This tough nut to crack lay between two ranges of hills, which made it, in effect, a gateway to the main part of Mexico.

What he would do when he got there, Old Rough-and-Ready did not know, though he must have pondered this problem many a time while he waited for those supplies.

Even if he crashed the gateway and saw all Mexico spread at his feet, it was about five hundred miles as the crow flies to the capital—and he was in no shape to fly like a crow. The between-land was all desert and high jagged mountains; there were no roads. A Mexican army could conceivably make a trip like that and finish it in fighting condition, but not an American army. Taylor had faith in his men, but he was not a fool.

Still, he had to go *somewhere*. He could not simply sit in Matamoros all summer. The people—and he was becoming very conscious of the American people—expected action from him.

July 6 he started up the Rio Grande.

CHAPTER

14

Voyage to Hell

MATAMOROS WAS A MESS, but undeniably an American mess. There was now a newspaper, *The American Flag*, privately owned and operated. There were sundry hotels and lunchrooms, and there was even a fountain selling "soda water with syrups." A daguerreotypist and a dentist, both from New Orleans, had opened shops. There was a theatre, two bowling alleys, and bars and brothels without number. Besides amateur shows, got up by the soldiers, the theatre housed a repertory company of professionals for a while, one of whom, a young man named Joseph Jefferson, opened a cigar store with his savings when the company went broke.

And volunteers kept pouring in all the time.

The flies were terrible, the fleas too, and the tainted water kept the tent-hospitals full. The days were hideously hot, and the nights, though cool, were infested by mosquitoes the soldiers swore were as big as birds: they used to call them "night hawks."

There was another kind of bar at the mouth of the Rio Grande, and it was called the Brazos de Santiago, which is to say, the Arms of St. James. It was only eight feet from the surface in high water, so most of the supplies, including the interminable volunteers who had not taken the time for any training, had to be lightered in. Soon, however, the steamboats began to come.

The first ones were privately owned and were there for commercial purposes: one operated daily between Matamoros and Point Isabel, for instance, the one-way fare being $3 deck passage, $10 with a cabin. The army boats, the boats Zachary Taylor had been clamoring for, followed these. They were all from the lower Mississippi and its tributaries, the Alabama, the Apalachicola, the Chattahoochee. They were small vessels, and most of them were not strong enough for the work they were to be called upon to do. Some drew as little as eighteen inches, unloaded, so that the Arms of St. James held no terrors for them. The deck hands and firemen were Mexicans, signed on locally. The officers were American civilians.

Not only the scouts attached to the camp at Matamoros but also the engineers appear to have been derelict in their duties. Somebody certainly should have examined those flimsy steamboats before they were sent upriver, loaded to the gunnels with men, materials, and cannon. The spring rise was still high, and the current strong, the Rio Grande being an exceedingly sinuous stream. There were only four vessels in the first fleet, and again and again one would take an hour or more struggling to get around a hairpin curve—only to pile up on the opposite bank when it had done so. They leaked. They were always having trouble with their rudders. Their mud drums were forever fouling. The fuel was green mesquit, and it was hard to get up much steam.

From Matamoros to Camargo, which was to be the jumping-off place for Monterey, was only a little over a hundred miles in a direct line, though there was no road. By river it was almost four hundred miles, and they did not dare travel after dark for fear of collisions.

When they got there they found that they were in hell. Matamoros had been bad enough, but at least the nights were cool. Camargo was not high enough to escape the desert's heat but it was far enough back from the Gulf so that the night's sea breezes did not caress it. The mosquitoes, however, were as bad, and the fleas, and the flies. There was as much dust, as much blowing sand. The tiny San Juan River, a tributary of the Rio Grande, was at once their sewer and their only source of drinking water. Cholera and dysentery soared to new highs, some of the companies having a third of their men on sick list all the time. These were good soldiers too, all regulars.

Commander Alexander Slidell Mackenzie was not noted for his common sense. He was best known to the public as the captain of the U.S.S. *Somers,* who on a cruise a few years earlier had hanged three members of his crew on charges of mutiny, one of them no more than a boy—being the son of the then secretary of war. Mackenzie had been tried for murder and acquitted. However, he did have good political connections, as his middle name attested, and he did speak Spanish.

Commander Alexander Slidell Mackenzie landed at Havana July 5, ostensibly to check rumors that the Mexicans were outfitting privateers there (they weren't), but actually in order to carry a secret message from President Polk to General Santa Anna. He was closeted with the distinguished exile for three hours, telling him that President Polk greatly desired peace and would meet appropriate commissioners for that purpose. The United States, he was authorized to say, would pay generously for any land it appropriated. What it most wanted, immediately, was a President of Mexico who could manage to stay President for a little while, one strong enough and sensible enough to take steps toward peace negotiations instead of falling back on the tired old hate-Yankees slogans.

He added that the United States Navy would not interfere with a return to Mexico on the part of Santa Anna, and in fact as a proof of good faith an order to that effect had already gone forth.

Santa Anna answered that the United States should threaten Monterey and if possible take it, and then press on and take Saltillo, a city somewhat farther south, nearer to the capital. At the same time the United States Navy would do well to bombard or at least to threaten Tampico and Vera Cruz. He even explained how this could best be done, for he was thoroughly familiar with both of those ports. *Then*, he pointed out, the people of Mexico would cry for a return of him, Antonio Lopez de Santa Anna; and the matter could be arranged.

He expected to be paid for all this, of course.[30]

He wrote out his reply, and Commander Mackenzie copied this, and Santa Anna destroyed the original, though the reason for all of this hush-hushness was not apparent, for anybody who knew the man could predict what Santa Anna would do, no matter what he had promised.

He did just that. He went to Vera Cruz, landed amid a somewhat ominous silence, and retired to one of his country places. It was necessary to wait, wetted forefinger held high, to determine which way the political wind was blowing. He soon learned that any move toward peace would ruin even his career, and that the attitude to take was anti-European, anti-monarchist, and most passionately anti-Yanqui. This he did, and he was soon recalled to the capital, a trip he pretended to be reluctant to make. After all, wasn't saving Mexico his calling in life, his métier, even though he never succeeded at it?

He raised money, somehow. He issued a fiery proclamation, calling upon all Mexicans to unite against the perfidious barbarians beyond the Rio Grande. He put himself at the head of the army.

Three days after Santa Anna landed at Vera Cruz,

THE TAKING OF MONTEREY

Zachary Taylor left Camargo for Monterey.

Monterey proved to be a tough nut indeed. A day of reconnoitering was followed by three days of furious fighting, most of it in the rain. The Mexicans, slightly superior in number, never gave an inch unless they were pushed hard. Outwork after outwork, fort after fort, had to be forced at the point of the bayonet, and the losses on both sides were terrible. Brigadier William Jenkins Worth, Taylor's second-in-command, led two thousand men in a long flanking movement that cut off the retreat road toward Saltillo; but the Mexicans fought on.

There was nothing brilliant about this battle, but it was dogged, soldiers against soldiers.

Late in the afternoon of the third day, when the northerners were taking the city house by house, having destroyed or overrun all of the outside fortifications, Taylor succeeded in bringing his big guns to bear against the cathedral. The Mexicans had their gunpowder stored there, enough to blow up the whole city. General Ampudia sent out a flag.

Taylor at first refused to treat on any other terms than unconditional surrender, but a look around caused him to change his mind. His men, drenched with rain, were scarcely able to stand, much less fight any further. The Mexicans were still well entrenched and would have to be prised out one by one at a terrible cost in casualties. Taylor was already running short of supplies. He had some five hundred dead to be buried soon, unless he risked a cholera epidemic, which could cost him all who remained; and there were the wounded to be cared for.

He granted an eight-week armistice, with the proviso that the Mexicans withdraw from the whole Rinconada valley, which would leave the road to Saltillo open. They could keep their muskets, but all cannons and munitions, together with the city itself, would become the property of the invaders. This armistice could be vetoed by either government at any time, in which case the general so commanded from home would notify the other general that hostilities were about to be resumed.

When they ran up the Stars and Stripes, and the band played "Yankee Doodle," the men had just about strength enough left to cheer,

CHAPTER

15

A Delicate Situation

THEY WERE CALLING this contest "Mr. Polk's War," but Mr. Polk himself was excruciatingly embarrassed by at least one aspect of it. A stern Presbyterian, he would not shirk his duty as commander-in-chief of the army and navy; but he was a stern Democrat as well, and it did begin to look as though the United States Army was officered entirely by Whigs.

Unlike the Mexican Army, which was studded with them like raisins in a raisin cake, the United States Army had never had many generals. The American people, since colonial times, had been instinctively leery of the trappings of militarism—the epaulettes, dress swords, sashes, regimental colors, honor guards—and generals, it would seem, typified these.

Even Zachary Taylor, at the time of his appointment as commanding officer in the southwest, had been only a brevet brigadier with the real rank of colonel. Since that time he had been promoted, though he was so little known in upper military circles that when Congress decided to honor him with a medal no one could find a painting or even a drawing of the man, and two artists were dispatched to Matamoros to see, and to record, what the general looked like.

There was Brigadier John E. Wool, hardly an inspired

—or inspiring—leader. He had been inspector general of the army for more than twenty years, and would have made the late Jean Martinet look sloppy. The troops called him "Old Granny," a nickname that had also been used for Horatio Gates in the American Revolution. Moreover, Wool was a pronounced Whig.

There was Major General Edmund Pendleton Gaines, a high ranker and a War of 1812 veteran, but he was in his dotage and his quarrels with his associates, both superior and inferior, had made him a laughingstock.[31]

There was Stephen Kearny, but he was needed in California. He had not been even a brigadier, anyway, when he started for the West. He did not get the commission until two days before he took Sante Fe.

And there was Winfield Scott.

This one at least *looked* like a general. He stood six feet four and was proportionately broad, without fat. He was handsome, even magnificent. The men called him "Old Fuss and Feathers," and as usual their designation was accepted by the public. Undeniably he did suggest a comic-opera character, and undeniably he did sometimes walk with what the irreverent were wont to call a turkey-gobbler's strut. But he knew his business. He was an authentic prodigy, who had covered himself with glory at Lundy's Lane, who had been brevetted a brigadier at the age of twenty-eight: he was now sixty. He had studied law, had traveled, and he possessed the manners of a man of the world, somewhat given to pomposity. But—not only was he an active Whig but he had gleaned a certain number of electoral votes in the 1840 and 1844 conventions and his ambition to be the Whig Presidential candidate in 1848 was an open secret.

The situation was complicated by General Taylor's string of victories. One of the reasons why he had been chosen for the post was because, as far as anybody knew, he had no politics. Now, suddenly, he was a hero, and men everywhere were organizing Taylor-for-President rallies.

James K. Polk was an American before he was a Democrat, though not very far before. He hated the thought of giving the Whigs *two* possible winners. He himself would not be available as the Democratic candidate, for he was committed to one term only, and he would gladly have given high commissions to prominent fellow party members, and did; but when it came to organizing an expedition to strike at the very heart of Mexico there simply was no Democrat in sight.

The President and his cabinet had decided upon nothing less than a descent upon the Mexican coast and an attack upon the capital, the much-touted halls of Montezuma. For months Zachary Taylor had been trying to tell them—and now at last they had decided that he was right—that it would profit nobody to flounder around any longer in northeastern Mexico, and that a strike from Monterey or Saltillo to Mexico City would be beyond the capabilities of any army the United States could presently put into the field. It was a matter of transportation. With a seacoast at its back, a coast patrolled by the United States Navy, an invading force could be kept supplied. It could not be so supplied across the mountains and forbidding deserts of central Mexico.

With this in mind, and perhaps also as a result of General Santa Anna's suggestion, the United States Navy, under Commodore David Conner, November 14, 1846, easily gulped Tampico. The proposed expedition, however, would be based at Vera Cruz, which might offer some resistance, and four days after Tampico was taken and garrisoned General Scott was formally invested with the command of that expedition.

He was not a man with whom it would be easy to get along. He insisted upon being treated with all the deference due to his rank. Polk disliked him. The two would never have agreed in any circumstances, for the one was expansive, the other reticent; the one was polished, the other crude. President Polk always had the feeling that General Scott was talking *down* to him, explaining the obvious in short, carefully pronounced words, like a schoolmarm addressing an especially stupid pupil.

Polk did not like or trust Zachary Taylor either, a feeling that was reciprocated. The President was shocked at the news of the armistice, and promptly ordered Taylor, through the Secretary of War, William Learned Marcy, to renew hostilities. Taylor thought that he had been rebuked, as in a sense he had. Like any soldier in the field, and rather more so than most of them, he was instinctively suspicious of the brass back home, the base boys; and he believed, not without reason, that he was about to be shelved in favor of the more flamboyant Winfield Scott.

Scott, like Taylor, had little use for the hordes of volunteers that kept pouring in. Like Taylor, he would place his principal faith on the regulars, whom he knew and whose discipline he could trust. But Taylor had the cream of the regulars, virtually all that could be spared. Scott must have these. As commander-in-chief he was entitled to them. As leader of a proposed attack against the enemy's capital he *had* to have them: you didn't do a job like that with militia and lately-outers. General Scott wrote to General Taylor, a polite letter, to tell him this. The reply was not very satisfactory, and so near the end of the year General Scott took ship for the mouth of the Rio Grande. He would go and get the regiments he wanted himself.

Santa Anna, President again, as well as commander-in-chief, was at San Luis Potosí, far to the south, approximately halfway between Monterey and the capital, and there he was performing miracles—this was the sort of thing he did best—in raising troops and money, making raw recruits into tough soldiers, and instilling them with enthusiasm. He was reported to have 25,000 men under him.

It was Santa Anna that General Taylor notified, November 5, that the armistice would cease to exist in eight days. On November 13, Taylor occupied Saltillo, still deeper into Mexican territory, farther from the Rio Grande and his bases. There was no opposition.

At Saltillo he was about two hundred miles due north of San Luis Potosí, but the intervening territory was grim. General Wool, who had started to invade Chihuahua, crossing the Rio Grande for that purpose, turned south to support Taylor instead, but the American forces in and around Saltillo still would be heavily outnumbered if Santa Anna came north. Nevertheless, Taylor moved still farther inland, in the direction of Victoria. Almost certainly he did this in order to avoid meeting Winfield Scott, who was coming from the north.

Scott landed at the Arms of St. James two days after Christmas and took one of those sleazy steamers up the Rio Grande and the San Juan to Camargo, where he had hoped to meet Zachary Taylor. Taylor was not there, and nobody seemed to know for sure where he was—somewhere in the direction of Victoria, probably.

Now, Winfield Scott was a gentleman, and he probably sensed that Zachary Taylor was trying to avoid him. His letters had been carefully written, and only once, when he ordered Taylor to stay on the defensive in the future, had he waxed in the least peremptory. Perhaps it was just as well that they did not meet; it surely would have been a painful episode, particularly so for Taylor. General Scott could not go on chasing General Taylor halfway across Mexico; he had other things to do. But it was important that General Taylor know exactly what regiments General Scott was taking—the best in the army—and why. General Scott sat down and wrote a long letter to General Taylor, making everything clear. He named the regiments he was detaching, and he pointed out that these would be used in an assault upon

Vera Cruz and later on Mexico City itself, an assault that would start very soon, in February or March.

This letter he sent by a captain to Zachary Taylor. It never got there. The captain fell into the hands of some Mexican bandits, who delivered the letter to Antonio Lopez de Santa Anna at San Luis Potosí.

The "Immortal Three-Quarters" must have given a long slow smile when this was translated for him. He was just about ready to move with his big army, and now he had two choices: he could go southeast to fortify Vera Cruz and the road up to the capital against the coming assault, or he could go due north, just about the same distance, to confront Zachary Taylor and his sadly weakened little army. He decided to do both, but the second first. He started north.

CHAPTER

16

'Twas a Famous Victory

SANTA ANNA departed from San Luis Posotí late in January. He did not command 25,000 men, as the popular report had it, but he probably did have close to that number. He had spent some months in hardening these men and equipping them, and he was at his best as a driver on the march. But the way was rugged and bare, and his losses were bad, from the very beginning. Men died of exhaustion. Men deserted. They were at all times weak from thirst. They staggered.

Once again it would seem that his scouts failed Old Zack, who never did have a fund for the secret hiring of spies and who in consequence was woefully ignorant of the movements of the enemy. Or it could have been a result of the clouds of cavalry Santa Anna sent out ahead of him. These were large parties, but very fast, and they traveled light. They were able to pick up more than one *norteamericano* scouting group, completely surrounding them so that not a man escaped.

At one time, when he was converging upon Victoria, the capital of the state of Tamaulipas, which offered no resistance, General Taylor was excitedly informed that Santa Anna with a huge army was marching straight for Monterey, which he was near. Taylor quickly doubled back and prepared for battle before Monterey, only to learn, after a few days of suspense, that Santa Anna wasn't doing any such thing, being still a good two hundred miles away.

His orders from Scott, relayed through lesser generals, were to fall back to Monterey and stand on the defensive there. He pointedly disobeyed these orders when he advanced upon Agua Nueva, his most southerly conquest so far, with the exception of Victoria, from which he had withdrawn.

Possibly because of the earlier false alarm Taylor did not believe them at first when they reported that Santa Anna really was coming this time, and he made no emergency preparations. It was not until February 20 that he learned for sure that Santa Anna and his legions had reached Encarnación, only about thirty miles away. This did not faze him, and he would have met the Mexicans right there, for he believed that any falling-back, however well advised from a technical military viewpoint, was bad for the spirits of the men; but his staff talked him into going back about eleven miles to a narrow field known by the Mexicans as La Angostura, or the Narrows,[32] a place much more easily defended.

Taylor had fewer than six thousand men at that time, and nine-tenths of them were volunteers who had never heard a shot fired in anger, and had not even been in Mexico very long. No Pointer himself, and certainly no "book general," Zachary Taylor knew the value of training, and he eyed the newcomers askance. There were some good men among them, no doubt, especially the officers, men like Henry Clay, Jr., of Kentucky, and Archibald Yell of Arkansas, and Jefferson Davis of Mississippi—talented amateurs, but they *were* amateurs; and you never knew how they might behave when the lead began to fly.

Santa Anna, though he had lost many on that terrible

march, must have had almost 20,000 men left, at least three times as big a force as Taylor's. He had twenty guns, big ones.

When he learned that the Yanquis were at Agua Nueva, a little over thirty miles to the north, Santa Anna decided to strike at once rather than give them a chance to retreat to a more suitable site. His men could scarcely stand, but he drove them all night, and they fell upon Agua Nueva at dawn.

There was nobody there. But there were ample evidences of a hasty departure—burned supplies, abandoned water bottles, and the like. But no Yanquis. They could not have gone far, and, as the President-General knew from that lovely letter of General Scott, they were largely raw troops. It would be easy to scatter them with a swift attack. He ordered his men on, and tired as they were they obeyed.

The spot selected for the confrontation was on (and on either side of) the road that went from San Luis Potosí to Saltillo. Paralleling this road, cutting the field almost exactly in half, was a north-running river—little more than a creek, really, but swollen at this season, for it had been an exceptionally wet winter. The rocky hills on either side, sharp-peaked like waves about to break, would be inaccessible to cannoneers, it was believed, and certainly inaccessible to cavalry units. The ground between the feet of these pinnacles and the road and the river was furrowed with empty, deep arroyos, or dry stream beds, and there again horsemen and artillery could not operate to advantage.

For immediate practical purposes this left only La Angostura, the Narrows, which was only a few hundred feet across. It was a veritable Mexican Thermopylae.

General Wool had picked the spot, and it was he who made the troop dispositions, General Taylor having gone on back with some Mississippians to look at the situation in Saltillo, which he had heard was threatened by a large Mexican cavalry force under General Miñon.

It was another cavalry force, the van of the main army, that came up the road from the direction of Agua Neuva the middle of the morning of February 22, Washington's birthday. It was headed by Santa Anna himself, and with it he hoped to smash the fleeing, frightened United States Army before the main part of his troops could even be drawn up for action. But he grounded to a stop, just out of range of the forward guns, when he saw the position at La Angostura. This was no frightened, fleeing army, but a calm, well-ordered, determined body, carefully placed, already dug-in, waiting.

By his chief medical officer, a Dr. Vanderlinden, Santa Anna sent a message to General Taylor, back from Saltillo, begging him to surrender and avert a bloodbath, for, this polite letter asserted, General Taylor's army was surrounded by more than 20,000 Mexicans. Old Zack's reply too was polite, and it was prompt. He regretted that he must "decline acceding to your request" to surrender.

This formality finished, both sides prepared for the killing to come.

It was a beautiful morning, sunny and cold. The Stars and Stripes flapped overhead, and a band was playing "Hail Columbia." Santa Anna sent out engineer scouts. This was too strong a position to be taken in one screaming sweep, as he had hoped to do.

Cannonading did not begin until the middle of the afternoon, and it was all at long range and for the most part ineffective. By that time the sun had gone and a drizzly rain was falling. La Angostura is six thousand feet above sea level, and it was bitterly cold that night. Most of the Americans had no tents, and none of the Mexicans had any, for they had raced ahead of their supplies. Nor was there any fire, on either side. This was not because either side sought to keep its position a secret but simply because there was not any firewood in that bleak countryside. A soldier without firewood is a pitiful object. It was a miserable night for

THE BATTLE OF LA ANGOSTURA—OR BUENA VISTA

both, but it must have been especially hard on the Mexicans, who after all had just marched forty-five miles in less than twenty-four hours with very little food and much less than that to drink.

The Yanquis did not dare to undress. They kept their guns with them, loaded. They did not even take the harness off the artillery horses.

The skirmishing of the late afternoon, all on the part of the Mexicans, who forced the fighting clear through, had been inconsequential, mere feints, feelings out, except for one large movement: Ampudia with a body of infantry that was being enlarged all the time as laggards caught up with the main army, was trying to outflank the *norteamericanos*' left by climbing the high crags on that side; but it was unlikely that his men could make it over that forbidding mass of rocks.

When dawn came, a dreary wet dawn, it was seen that Ampudia somehow *had* done it; his men lined the heights, frowning down upon the Yanqui flank.

This was a bad beginning.

Santa Anna had all his regimental buglers blow reveille at slightly different times, to give the barbarians from the north the impression of a vast multitude; and indeed, despite massive desertions, he still had at least three times the number of the Americans. Colors were paraded out there. Priests, scattered across the plain, celebrated mass after mass.

Grim, gaunt, the Americans waited.

They did not have to wait long. With the coming of full daylight the guns began banging. This was to be, like Monterey, a soldiers' battle, a slugfest. Taylor did not come into it until about nine o'clock, having been in Saltillo overnight, and he took little part in the actual struggle. He approved of the position Wool had chosen and of the dispositions that Wool had made. "Give 'em hell," he ordered now and then. For the most part he sat his horse in the very center of the line, by the side of General Wool, who did most of the supervising. There, scorning the bullets that whistled past (though some of them clipped his clothes), he sat with one leg hoisted up on the pommel of his saddle, Old Rough-and-Ready astride Old Whitey next to Old Granny. The men cheered.

As it had been the previous day, but on a much larger scale, the Mexicans forced the fighting. Again and again they charged, and again and again they were thrown back. It was often a near thing.

The volunteers, unexpectedly, did a good job. There were touches of panic, some desertions—a considerable group ran back to Saltillo, crying out that it was all over—and there were instances of confusion and of miscarried orders; but on the whole the volunteers did what they were told to do and did it very well. The regulars, all artillerymen, really shone. They would hold their ground until the charging Mexicans got almost to the muzzles of the cannons. Their officers, mostly young men fresh out of West Point, men like Captain John M. Washington, and Lieutenants

John Paul Jones O'Brien, George H. Thomas,[33] and Braxton Bragg, were superb, brilliantly puncturing the contention of certain congressmen that the United States Military Academy was not worth the money it cost the country.

Nothing was decided, and nothing new was introduced. There were no geniuses present, only heroes. When the day ended—and it had been a long day and a bloody one—the two sides were in just about the same position as they had been in the beginning.

The rain was no longer a mere drizzle. It was pouring now, a cloudburst, and the wind had knives.

Officer after officer that night went to General Taylor to plead for a retreat. The men just couldn't take it any more, they said. Taylor refused even to consider such a thing. The men could take it, and they would, he said.

Throughout the night they could hear sounds from the Mexican camp. There were still no fires, there still being no wood, but there were snatches of song, a creaking of harness, the thud of ration boxes, cries from sentries: "*Sentinela alerte!*" But when the sun rose—the rain had ceased—it gleamed upon a mere handful of men arranging for those sounds. At a distance it gleamed too upon the backs of the Mexican rear guard.

The battle was over.

It had been expensive. Taylor had lost 267 men killed, 456 wounded, 23 missing. The Mexican losses were not known, though they must have been much larger, since the Mexicans had fought hard, on the offensive all the time, assaulting entrenched positions. They left about 500 corpses on the field. Santa Anna would have had a mutiny on his hands if he had tried to drive those men any further.

Taylor did not even start to pursue. He gave his men three days of rest, and then he marched south again, retaking Agua Nueva, so that everything was back to where it had started.

Chapter

17

Army and Navy Together

THE MALADY THAT MEDICAL MEN call Leptospira icteroides, the rest of us yellow jack, comes suddenly. The head and loins ache, the flesh is sensitive, the victim feels drowsy. Then he gets acute stomach pains, and starts vomiting black stuff—that's why the Mexicans call it *el vomito negro*—while his skin grows orange-red and later a pallid green, the whites of his eyes turn yellow, his gums bleed, and he has an insatiable thirst. Sometimes too his nose bleeds and his face becomes smeared with clotted blood. Always he stinks. Death usually comes the fifth or sixth day, but if the patient does survive he faces a long, slow, painful, and messy recovery period marked by jaundice.

It was against this that Winfield Scott raced. Vera Cruz, True Cross, a walled city, which he must take before he could venture inland toward the capital of Mexico, was one of the yellow fever pestholes of the world, along with New Orleans and Cadiz. It had all the qualifications, being low, hot, dirty, and a seaport. Yellow fever was endemic there. It came with the summer, and came early. The regular inhabitants were enured to it, most of them actually immune because of previous exposure; but if an army of young men who had never before been in a hot country were to be kept there as late, say, as the middle of April, it could well cease to exist *as* an army. Whatever survivors there might be assuredly would be in no condition to climb mountains and fight battles. Scott knew he must beat the summer. He must take Vera Cruz and get up to the higher altitudes before the pestilence struck.

He knew this, and he toiled mightily to complete his preparations and sail south. The dour, louring President complained in his diary that Scott's "inordinate vanity" was the cause of leaks about the expedition and all sorts of delays, but in fact the general was doing everything possible to hurry the start.

Polk did not make matters any pleasanter when he tried to snatch Scott's command away from him. The general had just sailed for New Orleans, from whence he would go to the Rio Grande and on to Camargo in his futile attempt to meet Zachary Taylor, when the President proposed to have his friend and fellow Democrat, Senator Thomas Hart Benton of Missouri, appointed a lieutenant general, something that the United States Army had never had before, though Benton at this time held only an honorary colonelcy. It was Polk's contention that the head of the expedition—who might, after all, be called upon to negotiate a peace—should be a man politically in accord with himself, the President. Also, though he did not say this in so many words, such an appointment would greatly enhance Benton's chances of getting into the White House. Polk therefore asked Congress to create the new rank. This Congress refused to do; but General Scott had heard of the business by this time and was, understandably, furious. As a soldier, he wrote to the President, he did not fear the enemy before him; but, he asked, was he to have to contend with an enemy *behind?*

Thus, in a spate of snarling, the expedition was launched.

Scott had 13,660 men when he sailed from occupied Tampico, by now, like Matamoros, a thoroughly Americanized town. The rendezvous was off the Lobos Islands on the Gulf coast of Mexico about two hundred miles north of Vera Cruz. Vessels by the dozen, by the score, assembled there. There were mistakes, of course, and there were delays, but nothing occurred to send the edgy commander into hysterics, and March 2 they left there, a sea of hulls and sails. Four days later, aided by a strong norther, they were off Vera Cruz.

This was the strongest fortified city in the western hemisphere, a city the Spaniards had held for a long while after the rest of Mexico was free, but there was something slightly medieval, a shade archaic, about its fortifications. The stronghold of San Juan de Ulúa sat on a small island out in the bay, and it had walls sixty feet high in places, but the French fleet a few years ago, in the "Pastry War," had shown what modern guns could do to these. General Scott had heard that since that time the fort had been greatly strengthened, and he was worried about it.

Ulúa protected the water side of Vera Cruz. The three land sides were protected by a series of forts connected with curtains made of stone, brick, and cement, walls 15 feet high, 2½ to 3 feet thick.

It was yellow jack that Scott chiefly feared, but at the last minute, just before the final putting-forth, it was smallpox, breaking out in a company of Pennsylvania volunteers, that nearly smashed the whole effort. Prompt steps were taken to tend the stricken, to get all the well ashore on one of the islands, and to fumigate the ship. It worked.

Scott had been in touch with the naval commander in those waters, David Conner, and had asked him to pick a good landing site. Conner had done so, and after the preliminary handshakings and congratulations he took Scott and all his generals and their principal aides out in the little unarmed steamer *Petrita* to scout the coast. They ran too close to Ulúa, and were bracketed with a pattern of cannon shots, not one of which, fortunately, hit—or the war might have been ended then and there.

Scott and his staff agreed with the commodore that the spot selected, Mocambo Bay off Sacrificios Island, 2½ to 3 miles southeast of the city, should make an ideal landing place.

The surf boats were brought out and inspected and launched. These had been specially built for the occasion under a rush contract, and came in three sizes so that they could be packed easily. The largest were forty feet long, twelve feet wide, four feet deep. The next were slightly smaller, so that they could be fitted into the first ones, and the next were smaller still, forming a "nest" of three, like Chinese boxes. All were double-ended and almost flat-bottomed, and they would take between fifty and eighty soldiers each, besides eight oarsmen. Forty-seven of these "nests," or 141 boats, had been ordered. Only sixty-five boats had arrived, but these would be made to do.

March 8 had been selected as the day, but a norther threatened and it was postponed. The northers along that coast sometimes blow for two or even three days at a time, without any pause, and they can play havoc with anchorages. This one, as it happened, did not develop, but most of the day had passed before the men could be sure of this.

March 9 was perfect, the sea a lake, the breakers trifling. The shore they faced was a series of tufted dunes, behind which, they had no doubt, the Mexicans were waiting in force. The only persons in sight were a few horsemen, lancers, but Commander Tatnall's "mosquito fleet" of light-draft steamboats armed with small cannons easily chased these away, using grapeshot. Thereafter the grapeshot was used

THE LANDING OF AMERICAN TROOPS NEAR VERA CRUZ

to pepper the space behind the sand dunes; but this bombardment would perforce cease when the dash for the shore began.

That was at eleven o'clock. The navy, quick to cooperate, had furnished oarsmen, and the boats were expertly handled as they raced for the beach, keeping in line. They rode the surf and rasped ashore, and the men tumbled out, wading, their muskets held high. Those muskets were not loaded—the flintlock was too tricky an apparatus to be trusted in such a movement—but all bayonets had been affixed, and the men had no doubt that they would be using them soon.

They ran across the beach toward the first line of sand dunes. They ran up those dunes, crouching, ready to die. They stopped at the top, as though aghast, and for some time they did not move. Then they turned and by means of arm-waving told their companions back on the fleet that nobody was there. They cheered, and the sailors and the soldiers still at sea cheered back.

Thousands watched this movement from the roofs of nearby Vera Cruz, and every one of them must have wondered, as did every man in the fleet, why the Mexican commander, General Juan Morales, had not seized upon this first and most obvious opportunity to spike the assault. The question was never to be answered.

That first wave of attackers was followed by a second in the middle of the afternoon, and a third after dark. More than 10,000, with their muskets and plenty of ammunition, with their blankets and two days of cooked rations, had been put ashore in a few hours—and not one of them had so much as barked his shins.

CHAPTER

18

The Big Blast

THE FLEAS WERE TERRIBLE. They were sand fleas, big ones, as persistent as weevils. The sand itself was not friendly. When a norther was blowing, which was about half the time, the sand stung faces like a million needles. It worked its way under clothing. It got everywhere. It even shredded the canvas of some of the older tents.

The men, however, remained in high spirits; and the same could be said of the men they fought.

Until this time the war had all been in the north, where Yankee soldiers had not formed a high opinion of the Mexicans *as enemies*. The peons they had encountered were anything but fierce. They appeared incapable of hatred, poor things. They did not seem much interested in the war, one way or the other. To them, with their Indian resignation, their Indian fatalism, a soldier in whatever uniform was a person to be avoided, and when one such was friendly and even offered to pay for the food he took they were astonished and pleased, no matter what flag he fought under.

The residents of Vera Cruz were different. They took the war seriously, and they cursed the Yanquis. The Vera Cruzians were more sophisticated than the peons of the north, and much more emotional—more martial, too. Most of them, at the first sign of danger, had quit the city for more suburban parts or for havens in the hills. About 2,000 remained, and these must be assumed to be the most fearless, the stoutest in spirit, of the population of the city. There were about twice that many soldiers within the walls, most of them local militiamen, in addition to the Ulúa garrison of 1,200. They had plenty of ammunition, plenty of food, and a sound water supply. Moreover, they still had confidence in their masters at Mexico City. They had been promised relief and they believed in that promise. Was not the great Santa Anna coming back crowned with fresh laurels? Would he not lift the siege?

Like Napoleon after Borodino, Santa Anna after Buena Vista had not led his troops back through a harrowing retreat but had pushed on ahead of them. He had captured a few fieldpieces, a few stands of colors, and he displayed these, seeing no reason why he should make public how many trophies he had *lost*. Instead, in every city he pronounced himself a victor, and the people, though they should have known better by this time, took him at his word.

The *norteamericanos* had heard this, the story of the crushing defeat inflicted upon Zachary Taylor, as soon as they landed outside of Vera Cruz, but it had no depressing effect upon their morale, for they simply didn't believe it. When they learned the truth they averred that it was what they had expected all the time. It just proved that you could never trust a greaser.

Commodore Conner, who had been having a bad time with his neuralgia, a few days after the landing was relieved by Commodore Matthew Perry, a brother of the hero of Lake Erie. Perry was every bit as helpful as Conner had been. There was not a touch of inter-service bickering. Some of the biggest guns in the semicircular seven-mile line of siege batteries Scott was setting up were navy guns, some of the best gunners navy men. A company of 180 Marines

A NIGHT SCENE DURING THE BATTLE OF VERA CRUZ

under Captain Alvin Edson had gone ashore at Mocambo Bay with the first attack wave, and they stayed ashore.

General Scott had three alternatives.

He could besiege the city. He had the sea side of it completely closed, and all he needed to do was face inland and hold off any relief column that might be sent from the capital. But this could take a long while, and there was no reason to think that the yellow jack would be late that year.

He could order a frontal assault upon whichever part of the walls looked the least strong. This would be a bloody affair for all concerned.

He could bombard the city, from land and sea at the same time, in the hope of cowing its present proud spirit. This would mean expense and widespread destruction, but on the whole it would probably prove the best way. He decreed it.

It had been March 9 when the first of the troops scrambled ashore, and the next day they began to land heavy supplies. But several northers intervened, so that it was March 22 before Scott had his siege lines fully drawn, his guns in place. All of this work had been observed from the city, though there was almost no interference. Now the general called upon the city to surrender lest he knock it to pieces. The answer was prompt, and it was emphatic. The answer was "no."

Scott opened up. The city immediately answered. The din was deafening. For two days and two nights it seemed as though the very earth was tearing itself apart. Everything shuddered. Everything jumped. Vera Cruz was literally ringed with artillery fire, for not only the land batteries but the guns of all the war vessels in the bay banged away without pause. It was blind, insensate fury on both sides, and very noisy, yet though some civilians were killed and even a few soldiers, there was in fact very little damage. Scott did not concentrate upon any one part of the city, but simply blanketed the place with steel.

March 24 the British, French, Spanish, and Prussian consuls resident in Vera Cruz sent a message to General Scott imploring him to stop the bombardment for the sake of the women and children. He answered sharply, reminding them that they had been given ample warning to leave the city and pointing out that the Mexican commanding officer had turned down an offer to abstain from bombardment. Any move toward bringing about a cease-fire, the general stated, would have to come from the said Mexican commanding officer.

This was shrewdly put, for the situation had changed, as Scott must have known. No longer could the Vera Cruzians expect help from the capital, where still another revolution was in the making, men shooting at one another in the streets. And the forty-eight hours of thud had shaken the spirit of the Vera Cruzians, who now pleaded for peace. The commanding officer, General Morales, resigned because of ill health. It could be that he really was ill; but it is noteworthy that this was a dodge common to the time and place, a way of getting out of blame for surrendering, and indeed it was almost in itself an order to the second-in-command, General Juan de Landero, *to* surrender. De Landero sent out a flag.

The commissioners sat up late Saturday night, March 27. The *norteamericanos* for some time held out against the granting of conditions, but the spectre of yellow fever was always at their shoulders, its fetid breath against the back of their necks, and soon they submitted to the Mexican demands for full honors of war.

The easiest thing they submitted to was the demand that the victors refrain from interfering in any way with the Vera Cruzian religious habits and practices and that they promise not to damage in any way the various churches, monasteries, and nunneries. They had never had any intention of doing anything like that anyway, of course; but the Mexicans seemingly believed or pretended to believe their own propaganda. Religion, to the northerners, had no part in this war. To the Mexicans it was a central issue. The Mexican leaders from the beginning had insisted that the Yanquis were on a crusade to wipe out the Roman Catholic Church, to rob the rich parishes, to kill the monks and priests, and, almost as an afterthought, to rape all the nuns.[34] It is not likely that the leaders themselves believed this, but it is certain that the populace did, and it is significant that it was one of the first things the Mexican armistice commissioners demanded.

The next day, Sunday, the commanding officers on each side verified the agreement.

The day after that, a lovely sunlit day with a fine southeast breeze to fill the flags, the actual capitulation took place.

It was done with dignity. Nobody was to be imprisoned, but the officers had pledged for themselves and for their men that none would take any further part in the war. The officers retained their side arms, but the rank and file stacked their muskets, surrendering them. When now and then a soldier, moved to tears, would try to smash his musket rather than give it up, he would not be restrained. There was no jeering, no gloating. The Mexicans were in their best uniforms, and they kept good order, marching up and marching away in perfect step, their heads high. Winfield Scott, who might have been expected to glory in this ceremony, was not even present. Major General William J. Worth, his second-in-command, formally accepted the surrender. The band played "Hail Columbia."

CHAPTER
19

In the Footsteps of Cortez

THERE WAS MUCH TO BE DONE. There were supplies to be landed, and storage plants to be built; there were reports to be made out, and requisitions; there was a proclamation to be posted, solemnly promising the public that the Roman religion would be in no way tampered with or hindered; there were licenses to be issued to enterprising American civilians who wanted to open grog shops—five of these in the first week of occupation; there were horses and mules to be purchased and shod, and wagons to be collected; there was a camp follower to be hanged, in public, after he had been found guilty of rape; and there was the men's health to worry about. What with all these things, and many more, it was not until April 6 that the first marching order was issued, April 8 that the vanguard set forth.

Of the way to be taken there had never been any doubt. A few miles along the beach north of Vera Cruz they would pick up the National Highway, a road paved, graded, and guttered by the Spaniards more than three hundred years earlier, and still in everyday use. It had not been maintained as well as under the Spaniards, but it remained a better road than most of the northerners had ever seen. It went to Jalapa, some four thousand feet above sea level, a city celebrated for its beauty, which was to be the first objective.

No serious interception east of Jalapa was expected.

The National Highway continued west of Jalapa to Puebla, the second largest city in Mexico, and then on to the capital itself, Mexico City, D.F. Undoubtedly they would run into trouble before they got *there*, though General Scott remained hopeful, as he wrote to Secretary of War Marcy, that somewhere along the way they would be met by a delegation proposing peace.

The first part of the way, over sand, on a day "excessively close and hot,"[35] was arduous, but soon they came to the colorful and fertile lands owned by the dictator himself, on both sides of the highway most of the distance between Vera Cruz and Jalapa, forty-odd miles, millions of acres; and this was much more agreeable.

On the third day they came upon the National Bridge, a showplace, and crossed the Rio del Plan to the Plan del Rio, which could be termed the dividing line between *tierra caliente* below and *tierra templada* above. They were, as a local saying had it, about to leave the land where reigned King Death in his Yellow Robe.

Santa Anna was there waiting for them.

Santa Anna had reorganized his army at San Luis Potosí, had left it drilling there, had gone on to the capital, where he more or less reconciled the two sides in the indeterminate revolution that was in progress by the simple method of asserting himself as dictator, and where he raised two million dollars and yet another army, with which he sallied forth to stop the invader in his tracks. Surely no other man in Mexico could have done so much in so short a time.

That Scott would move along the National Highway was taken for granted. Some of the wiry Mexican Indian infantrymen might have made it cross-country, traveling light, but for an army with cavalry, artillery, and all its own supplies this would be unthinkable. The question was: Where to lie in wait for him?

A Crusano himself, the President-General was familiar with every foot of the way; indeed, he *owned* much of it, the most important part. He knew that General Scott feared yellow jack more than he feared any living man, and his first thought was to keep the invaders down in the low seaboard region, the pestilential region. There were sundry possible places, but he chose Cerro Gordo largely because, except for the National Bridge, which it would have been difficult to fortify, it was the easternmost of these places, the one, that is, nearest to the sea, the lowest.

He was to be much criticized for this choice, but it looked like a good one at the time. Cerro Gordo ("Thick Hill") was an eight-hundred-foot bulbous eminence between the National Highway and the Rio del Plan, both of which it could easily control, though the river was not navigable anyway. It was about twenty miles east of Jalapa. It was flat on top, an acre or so of clear space, and was sometimes called El Telegrafo from the square stone signal tower the Spaniards had erected there many years earlier as part of a Vera Cruz-to-Mexico City fire signal system.[36] This hill was heavily gunned and heavily manned.

Half a mile to the northeast was another hill, Atalaya, not quite as high, not cleared on top, and with thickly thicketed sides. Santa Anna stationed a mere handful of musketeers and a few guns on Atalaya because its northern side, the side that faced the National Highway along which the invaders must come, was exceedingly steep and so covered with chaparral that, as the President-General himself put it, a rabbit couldn't get through.

These two hills formed his left wing. His center was his camp and the tiny village of Cerro Gordo on the banks of the Rio del Plan. His right was three outstretching rocky promontories each of which was well fortified at its farthest tip, facing the way the enemy must come.

The enemy came April 12, and the leader of the first division, Brigadier General David E. ("Old Davy") Twiggs, who was in temporary command of the whole column during the illness of Major General Robert Patterson, proposed to assail the position right away. His aides persuaded him that the men were too weary after a long march, and he consented to wait until the next day. Apparently it never occurred to him to have the place reconnoitered.

Next day General Patterson took himself off the sick list, reassuming command, and ordered that there should be no advance, no decisive action of any sort, until General Scott arrived on the scene.

Scott was on his way. Though James K. Polk in faraway Washington fretted about his slowness in action, which Polk attributed to an overemphasis on "book tactics," Winfield Scott could go fast when speed was called for. At present, in Vera Cruz, his greatest problem was transportation. Moving men was not difficult; but moving supplies was. Something between thirty-five and forty of the small vessels bringing goods from the States had been wrecked or driven aground by northers, and it happened that most of these were loaded with draft animals—horses or mules or both. It had been in Scott's original plan to get a large part of his pullers from the territory around Vera Cruz, and especially from the fertile Alvarado River valley, but raids of these places had yielded little.

Sending the greatest part of his army toward Mexico City meant sending supply trains after them, and every supply train had to be guarded not against the Mexican regulars but against the bandits who swarmed over that part of the country.

Scott was astounded when he learned that Santa Anna

had somehow gathered together yet another army. The reports had the dictator with anywhere from three thousand to nine thousand men. Even the lowest figure would have been a formidable force encamped in a pass like that of Cerro Gordo. Winfield Scott decided that this called for his personal attention. He started for the front.

He arrived at the United States encampment on the Plan del Rio at about noon April 14, and he promptly sent out three of his brightest young aides, each of whom had been an honor man at the Point in his time, to reconnoitre. These were Captain Robert E. Lee and Lieutenants Pierre Gustave Toutant-de Beauregard and Zealous B. Tower.

They took a good look; and they reported back that they believed the Mexican left flank could be turned. If this was done—and the hardest part would be to get the guns over, a task assigned to Lee—the road to Jalapa would be cut and both Mexican flanks would be pinned against the Rio del Plan. This stream was not wide but it was fast and it ran in a deep, steep-sided gully.

The U.S. left was to advance upon the three fingers of the Mexican right as soon as it heard firing from upstream —firing, it was hoped, that would signal the cutting of the road to Jalapa. This was supposed to be little more than a holding action, and it was committed to the command of Brigadier General Gideon J. Pillow, a man who owed his commission to the fact that he had helped his fellow Tennesseean James K. Polk win the Democratic presidential nomination, and who was not considered a military genius.

Captain Lee and the men under him performed prodigies of movement, amazing a more obscure young officer, Lieutenant Ulysses S. Grant, who watched them:

> The walls were so steep that men could barely climb them. Animals could not. . . . The engineers, who had directed the opening, led the way and the

troops followed. Artillery was let down the steep slopes by hand, the men engaged attaching a strong rope to the rear axle and letting the guns down, a piece at a time, while the men at the ropes kept their ground at the top, paying out gradually. . . . In like manner the guns were drawn by hand up the opposite slopes.[37]

Old Davy Twiggs was leading his men along the highway just north of Atalaya, following those guns, when they were seen and fired upon from the top of the hill. Instead of running away, they ran *at* the hill. Rabbits might not be able to get through, but *they* did. The cannoneers could not depress their pieces enough to reach them as they climbed, while the musketeers—shooting down is always harder than shooting up—fired too high. Twiggs's men, led by redheaded Colonel William S. Harney, tore through the chaparral and got to the top unhit. Nobody was there. The greasers had skedaddled, abandoning their guns.

Excited, their blood up, Harney's men chased the foe right down the south side of the hill, which was much less steep than the north side, and almost halfway up the neighboring hill, Cerro Gordo. There they were pinned down by heavy fire and had to take cover, from which they did not dare to break until after dark.

The Mexicans cheered, for they thought that the *norteamericanos* were retreating.

In the morning, a Sunday, April 18, 1847, they learned the truth. Harney's men tried it again. At seven o'clock, yelling like maniacs, they ran down the south side of Atalaya, across the intervening hollow, and up the north side of Cerro Gordo. Two-thirds of the way up they threw themselves flat on the ground in order to get some breath back, but in a few minutes they sprang to their feet again and ran on. There was some fighting at the top, but not much. Most of the Mexicans ran, spreading panic among those in the

The Battle of Cerro Gordo

camp below. The Yanqui gunners turned the still-hot guns upon that camp; a sergeant named Thomas Henry pulled down the Mexican flag on the *telegrafo* tower and ran the Stars and Stripes up in its stead; and the others, after catching their breath, started down the south slope of Cerro Gordo.

At about this same time Bennett Riley's brigade came charging around the northern side of that hill, and a few minutes later Brigadier Shields's men, incredibly equipped with heavy guns, came tearing out of the tangle to the north.

It was a real rout. There was almost no attempt at resistance, nor was there anybody to try to rally them, for Antonio Lopez de Santa Anna ran with them, among the first.

The cavalry did not pause to cover the retreat but galloped on ahead—to the west. These were not the best troopers in the Mexican Army, which had always been proud of its cavalry. Santa Anna had scraped the bottom of the barrel.

They did not stop until they had reached Orizaba, more than thirty miles southwest of the field of battle, if battle it could be called.

Gideon Pillow's attack upon the Mexican right wing had gone sour, but this was not important. That wing was pinned down anyway. Its members could hear the shouts of victory, could hear the panic, the beginnings of a disorderly retreat. They knew that they were doomed. They raised a white flag.

Nobody ever took the trouble to count them, but it was estimated that there had been about four thousand persons in that right wing, of which about a thousand slipped away in the excitement before they could be herded into one place. Winfield Scott released them all on parole in the custody of their officers, who included five generals. He had no place to put them, and he could not possibly have fed and otherwise cared for such an enormous addition to his army. Also, he hoped that this action, which would be much talked about, would encourage other Mexicans to quit early in the fight, assuming that there was any further fighting.

The battle plan had gone wrong inasmuch as the road to Jalapa had not been cut, trapping the whole Mexican force, including Santa Anna himself. Nobody had expected the Mexicans to run so soon. Nevertheless, Cerro Gordo had been a stunning success. The loot included thousands of Brown Bess muskets, which were smashed as being no good to the United States Army, hundreds of tents, mountains of supplies, vast quantities of ammunition, a military chest containing most of the $2,000,000 Santa Anna had managed to raise, about forty brass cannons, which were spiked and thrown into the river, and scores of regimental flags and other trophies.[38]

And—the road to Mexico City was open.

CHAPTER

20

A Jar of Marmalade

To the victor belongs the headache. Winfield Scott was a bitter, bitter man, a frustrated man. No general ever thinks he has enough troops for the task on hand. The call for reinforcement comes as naturally to such a personage as breathing. Scott had said that he would need 20,000 men for the thrust to Mexico City. He had about 12,000 when he landed near Vera Cruz, and at no time was he to command more than 14,000, of whom about 2,000 would be on sick list. At Jalapa and at Perote, both of which he occupied a few days after Cerro Gordo, making his headquarters at the former, he had about 8,000 men, about 1,000 of them sick.

He had just heard from the War Department that the brigade under John Cadwalader, a Philadelphia lawyer, which was to have been sent to Vera Cruz, had been diverted instead to the army of Northern Mexico. He howled, in a letter to Marcy, that this could only mean that the Polk administration had set out to "ruin" him, which was preposterous. (Actually, the alarm that had brought about this diversion had proved to be a false one, and Cadwalader and his men even then were on their way to Vera Cruz, but Scott did not know this.)

He had just lost a sizable body of Irishmen, Roman Catholics whom the Mexicans through spies had induced to desert, just as a similar body of men had deserted from Taylor's army at Matamoros. These were combined as the San Patricio corps, an artillery unit.

What was even worse, the twelve-month volunteers, who comprised almost half of his army, were about to leave. Their time was up. Major efforts to induce them to sign for the duration had failed. Except for a handful, they insisted that they be sent home as promised, and it was necessary for General Scott, with all the other things he had to do, to arrange that they be got down to the coast and shipped off. The terms of the various units expired anywhere from late May until the middle of July, and in all that time the yellow fever could be assumed to be raging in Vera Cruz. Nevertheless, the men must go.

Manpower, then, was Scott's first worry. As he advanced toward Mexico City his line to his base increased and it had to be patrolled all the time. Moreover, as he took over towns and cities and strongholds—Jalapa, Puebla, Perote—he had to garrison them; he could not leave them unguarded.

At this most inauspicious of all possible moments there appeared on the scene a sickly, gangling, querulous, cadaverous officeholder, the chief clerk of the Department of State, Nicholas P. Trist. He wrote to General Scott from Vera Cruz, asking him—commanding him, rather—to send on to President-General Santa Anna the enclosed message. You did not address Winfield Scott in this fashion, and, besides, the enclosure was sealed. The General almost had a fit.

"Chief clerk" suggests some humble, ink-stained wretch of a pen-pusher. This, Trist was not. He had attended West Point, though he had not been graduated. He had studied law. He had served as personal secretary to President Andrew Jackson. He had served two years as the United States consul at Havana, where he learned Spanish. Married to a granddaughter of Thomas Jefferson, he was the Number-two man in the State Department, in effect the undersecretary, though that title did not exist.

Now, General Scott himself had proposed that a diplomat be sent to the field, somebody authorized to treat with Mexican peace commissioners in case any such were appointed. He had expected, of course, to be so authorized in his own right, but he would have welcomed a trained State Department official who could give him advice about details. Most certainly he had *not* expected to be ordered around like an office boy. He answered scathingly, refusing to forward the enclosure because, he said, there wasn't any real Mexican government. He sent a copy of this letter to his superior, Secretary of War William Learned Marcy. It was a plot, he asserted, to "degrade" him.

He had been wrong about the Mexican government. It existed, though it was even more shaky than usual. Undoubtedly there were in the capital, in the Congress, men who would gladly have taken steps to bring about a peace —if they had dared. The politicians were sick of the whole business and they knew that they could not win, but the people, or at least a voluble portion of them, still breathed martial sentiments. Congress wanted to get Santa Anna to take the first steps, and *he* wanted *it* to do so. This was the time of all times to start to treat. But Winfield Scott and Nicholas P. Trist couldn't be bothered with such an affair. They were too busy calling one another names.

Trist, in the midst of an impressively large cavalry escort, went up to Jalapa. He did not attempt to call upon General Scott, and this was just as well for Scott almost certainly would have refused to receive him. Trist, indeed, appeared to think that the *General* should first call on *him*. Thus, neither side moved.

Trist took two days and two nights to write a thirty-page explanation of his attitude and his authority. Scott did not even stoop to read it, but in the presence of a large number of officers that night he had it read aloud. Next day he wrote to Trist that he had found the statement "a farrago of insolence, conceit, and arrogance." He sent a copy of this letter to Secretary of War Marcy, as Trist had sent a copy of *his* letter to Secretary of State James Buchanan.

In Washington there was consternation. President Polk called a special meeting of the cabinet to consider the situation. He himself was in favor of removing Scott, but the others dissuaded him from this on the ground that it would wound the morale of men so deep in Mexican territory.[39] The two secretaries involved, however, were instructed to write forceful reprimands to their respective underlings. Meanwhile, six weeks had been lost.

Scott's van had taken over Puebla readily enough, and the general himself soon followed, as did Nicholas P. Trist. These two still were not talking to one another. The officer to whom Trist had been attached, Brigadier General Persifor Smith, was a tactful man—in civilian life he was a judge —and he tried to smooth the ruffled feathers. Another engaged in this laudable occupation was Edward Thornton, fresh out of Cambridge and *attaché* at the British embassy in Mexico City.[40] The British government early in the war had offered its services as a mediator, and though neither side had formally accepted this offer the new foreign minister in Mexico City had approached the British ambassador, Charles Bankhead, who had sent his assistant to the United States lines. But Thornton could do little while the general and the chief clerk remained at loggerheads. He returned several times.

The trouble was that the only man who could swing a peace deal—if he dared—was Antonio Lopez de Santa Anna, whose prestige wobbled. Santa Anna said he needed a million dollars with which to buy votes in the Congress, a standard practice in Mexico City at the time. Neither Scott nor Trist had authority to pay such a sum, even if they had possessed the cash; nor could the deed be done except by Congress, which would have meant a major scandal. Scott did have a slush fund, brought along for this very purpose, and he did offer to pay Santa Anna $10,000 out of this; but nothing came of the business.

It was the general who broke off the feud. That was on July 4, and the troops in Puebla were celebrating, which perhaps induced in him a mellow mood. At any rate, hearing that Nicholas P. Trist was ill, Scott fished out a jar of guava marmalade and sent it to Persifor Smith to be given to the patient. It happened that the chief clerk loved marmalade, and a reconciliation quickly followed. After that, they worked well together; and each wrote to his respective department taking back what he had said about the other and requesting that the pertinent letters be removed from the file.

It had been Scott's first impulse after Cerro Gordo to go in prompt pursuit of Santa Anna and keep him off balance. He had not been able to do this because of the shortage of men. Cadwalader's reinforcement had reached him at last, but he well knew that he commanded only about one-third of the forces that Santa Anna had gathered in Mexico City, an extraordinarily strong spot. Still, he couldn't stay where he was. August 7 he moved out of Puebla, making for the Valley of Mexico.

There was a storm of criticism, to which the general paid no attention. In England the great Duke of Wellington shook his head when he heard the news. "Scott is lost," he said. "He can't take the city, and he can't fall back upon his base." [41]

CHAPTER

21

The Dream City

TWO THINGS ABOUT MEXICO amazed the soldiers—the mountains and the cigarettes.

Some of them had seen mountains before, but nothing like these majestic peaks. In the north the terrain had been largely desert or bare dun prairie, and along the Gulf coast it was sandy, steamy, hot, though even there on a clear day you could see the iridescent sides of Orizaba; but once they had passed Jalapa, that garden city, and attained the great central plain, they were met by all the heights of Mexico the magnificent—Popocatepetl, Malinche, Ixtaccihuatl. They had never known that such things existed, and they never tired of staring at them.

The *cigarito*—the boys soon shortened that to "cigarette"—was different. It hardly inspired awe, though it never failed to create astonishment. The cigarettes were like tiny cigars, only the shredded tobacco was rolled in a piece of white paper or, sometimes, a corn husk. It was odd enough when the men smoked these funny little things, but it was astounding when the women did—at home in their windows, on the street, at the marketplace. The soldiers were not shocked; they thought the sight a rather pretty one, but it never failed to give them a jolt. Many bought packages of these "cigarettes" to take home as souvenirs, though it was generally agreed that the habit would never become popular in the States.

He who hesitates is not necessarily lost. Had not Scott waited for the arrival of 2,400 soldiers under Franklin Pierce August 6, together with all of their pack animals and all their supplies, he must surely have been overwhelmed before he could reach the Valley of Mexico. As it was, he started out early the next morning, a Saturday. He had a little over 10,000, though he left many hundreds of sick behind.

Moreover, the time had not been entirely wasted. Scott's engineers, those brilliant Pointers, the best he commanded, had been drawing maps of the Valley of Mexico. Not one of them had even *been* there, but they relied upon the accounts of Mexicans in Puebla who had; and the results, when put to the proof, were to show uncannily accurate.

The capital sits in a shallow depression about 46 by 32 miles, ringed with mountains, studded with lakes, roughly 7,500 feet above sea level. It may have been a huge volcanic crater thousands of years ago. It was largely water, a vast lake, stippled with islands, when Cortez first saw it. Much of this had been filled in, but six large lakes remained. The place was a natural fort. Mexico City, in its center, was about 75 miles from Puebla.

The hesitation was not all on one side. Mexico City was in a state of near-anarchy. The Puros and the Moderatos, together with a dozen splinter parties, were scrambling for power, stepping on one another's faces, stabbing one another's backs. The constitution had just been amended twice, suddenly, violently. Congress, torn from within, could no longer get a quorum. There was shooting in the streets. Many of the outlying states, which never had evinced any love for the Federal District, were striving now to evade

The Dream City 147

their obligations to send troops, and some were practically in a state of revolt. In the northwest, for example, Sonora, Sinaloa, and Durango had formed what amounted to an independent republic; California and New Mexico were gone, probably forever, largely because of enemy action; and Zacatecas and Yucatan, as usual, were staying aloof. Every able-bodied man between the ages of fifteen and sixty was supposed to be in arms, but they were not. Desertions, despite savage punishments, were on a grand scale. The only stable quality, just at first, seemed to be Antonio Lopez de Santa Anna. The truth about Buena Vista had come out, and the truth about Cerro Gordo could never be hidden, so that the people as a whole disliked and distrusted the President-General, and they wanted him to stay out of the capital, and told him so; but he had the most soldiers, and he was still Santa Anna. Yet he himself seemed woefully bewildered. When he learned that he was not wanted in Mexico City he decided—at great personal sacrifice, to hear him tell it—that he would resign the Presidency. A few hours later he took back that resignation. Soon afterward he resigned again, and then he withdrew *that* resignation. Because Congress was impotent, he became again a dictator. He and he alone, he said, could save Mexico.

In the malodorous purlieus of Vera Cruz the invaders had found little of Mexico to admire,[42] but as they went west this changed and they became filled with wonderment. Jalapa was a pretty spot; Perote, like San Juan de Ulúa, an almost unbelievably picturesque medieval stronghold;[43] but it was Puebla that left them gasping. Few of them, unless they had visited Philadelphia or Washington, had ever before seen a *planned* city; many, indeed, had never seen a city at all, excepting briefly the seaports of New Orleans and Vera Cruz. The perfectly laid-out streets of Puebla and its massive cathedral and kingly plaza never failed to fascinate them, and they would wander about by the hour, gawking. Still more stunning was the realization that they were headed for the republic's pearl among cities, the fabled capital itself. This was like getting an invitation to visit the Hanging Gardens of Babylon.

The Pueblans were less enthusiastic about what they saw. Indeed, they were downright disappointed. Tall tales had been told about these *norteamericanos*, especially since Cerro Gordo, and it was expected that they would be truly gigantic; but in the event they were only of average size, and slouchy to boot. A soldier should glitter; these were drab, dusty. Excepting for the splendiferous figure of the general himself—and he seldom went out-of-doors—it was an army virtually without gold braid, all untasselled. Not only did it fail to violate the nunneries and rob the altars in its course, it didn't steal *anything*. It would stir no Mexican heart.

The way was miry. It had been an exceptionally dry summer, as summers went in that part of the world, but there was still a great deal of mucilage-like mud, so that rolling the guns and keeping the pack animals on the move was hard work. The men were spurred, however, by the expectation of seeing that dream city in the Valley of Mexico.

There was little annoyance besides the mud. Bands of cavalry had been instructed to harass the invaders, but they kept a careful distance. Groups of irregulars had been organized and sent out into the field, but they dabbled in banditry, leaving the armed *norteamericanos* alone. The villagers along the route had been told to hide things from the northern barbarians, but they soon learned that it was better to sell food to these curiously colorless soldiers than to leave it to be stolen by the *bandidos*.

In a few days the troops were surmounting the outer rim of the Valley of Mexico, seeing below them as they did so the famous lakes, the city itself, and many thousands of enemy soldiers. There was no resistance at the rim.

Santa Anna's plan was simple, and it was to be adversely criticized as unimaginative, but he had no great trust in the troops he commanded, raw levies for the most part, and after all time was on his side. If he could just dig in and hold off whatever attacks the *norteamericanos* would make—that in itself might end the war. For Scott had indeed broken away from his base, and if he did not get fresh supplies soon his army would dissolve, disperse, scatter. Men may be ever so valorous, but when they get hungry they go looking for food. Santa Anna knew this. Why should he concoct an elaborate pattern of defense? All he needed to do was sit tight.

The logical place to attack, the nearest and most direct, was the Peñon Viejo, a high point which the Mexicans had fortified and heavily garrisoned. If he went in a straight line for the capital Scott would be obliged to pass close to Peñon Viejo, but to take the place by a frontal attack—and there was no other way—would be exceedingly expensive of men. Moreover, Santa Anna, occupying a position in the middle of the circle, could reinforce any part of the perimeter in less time than it would take the invaders to shift position. The Peñon Viejo lay between two of the biggest lakes, Xochimilco and Texcoco. After studying it for several days, Scott decided against an assault. However, he kept a large force there in a threatening posture.

To their left, as they stood facing Peñon Viejo, was a fantastic field of black twisted rocks, lava from Ajusco, a nearby volcano, which had been there as far back as the memory of man could stretch. This was called the Pedregal, or Place of Rocks. Pack animals could not traverse it, nor could cannons, but men on foot, carrying all their own gear, could make a painful way through it. Some of the men thought that it looked like a storm-tossed sea frozen into black rock, the usual metaphor, but one lad remarked that it looked like hell with the fires out.

Scott elected to go south of the Pedregal, south too of sprawling Lake Chalco with its mushy shores, a route that Santa Anna's engineers had pronounced impassable. It was a left hook that landed him, August 19, on the road to Acapulco, a road that proceeds directly south from the capital city at this point. He started up that road, though all the time he was menacing Peñon Viejo to the east.

Santa Anna quickly reinforced his army south of the city, and ordered the southernmost force under General Valencia to join him. Valencia, a gorilla of a man with ferocious mustachios and almost no neck, chose to disobey the order. He believed that he could stop the northern barbarians in their tracks, and he too had his eye on the Presidency.

There followed two days of confused fighting, not so much an organized battle as a series of catch-as-catch-can brawls, all of them fierce. The first day was rainy and indecisive. The second was clear and cold, and an emphatic United States victory. Valencia was smashed, his army badly mauled. The man himself fled.

It was a field officers' show, with very little generalship on either side. It was a soldiers' fracas, a slugfest. The Mexicans did better than anyone had expected them to, though eventually they surrendered or ran away.

Immense stores of supplies, muskets, and ammunition had been captured, together with more than 70 brass cannons. The Mexican prisoners numbered 2,637, including eight generals and two past Presidents. And the road to the capital was open.

CHAPTER

22

Sober Men and True

THE WAR SHOULD HAVE BEEN OVER. As soon as the fighting was broken off, and even before the dust had settled, Scott could have marched his men right into Mexico City. There were several reasons why he didn't.

In the first place, the men were dog-tired. Most of them, the members of the main force, had fought indecisively but savagely all of the previous day, had sat up shivering, without tents, in an icy rain all night, and had started to fight again at dawn. They were in no condition to conquer a foreign capital, even though it seemed to be offered on a silver tray. There could well be street fighting, the dirtiest kind. It was late afternoon, and night falls swiftly in that clime—with a click, as in the tropics.

Winfield Scott was bluff, as a soldier should be. He saw things in black and white, and the positively Oriental tergiversation of a Santa Anna was more than he could comprehend. While still at Puebla he had been given to believe that Santa Anna would gladly surrender if the Yanquis won a battle that brought them to the city gates; and this had happened, and he expected to hear from the President-General at any time now.

Neither had he forgotten that the next year was a Presidential election year back home. He wanted to make a good peace—for he was essentially a good man—a lasting, just peace. To scoop up the capital would be a glorious thing, a thing that would shine very bright at home, virtually making that Whig nomination a certainty; but it might be a damned bloody thing as well, and he was down to only about seven thousand effectives. Besides, the general expected to see a white flag at any minute now, and he had already prepared a summons to the city to surrender.

An informal delegation of Britishers sought him out that very night—Thornton the attaché, whom he had met several times back in Puebla, and the consul general in Mexico City, a man named Mackintosh, who represented a commercial firm with large Mexican interests and was himself married to a Mexican. The session was secret, but there could be no doubt that these men urged a move for peace. They handed Scott a letter from the Minister of Foreign Affairs, Ramón Pacheco, a carefully worded missive addressed to Secretary of State Buchanan and purporting to be an answer to Buchanan's earlier letter sent by Trist—the one Scott for a time would not transmit. This was done, Pacheco added informally, because of a recently passed law making it a capital offense to treat in any way with the enemy. The letter was really for Scott, and he read it. The word "peace" was not used, but an immediate cease-fire was implied.

Next morning, early, as Scott was moving his headquarters from little San Agustín to the archbishop's palace on a hill at Coyoacan, much nearer to the center of things, he was approached by General Ignacio Mora y Villamil, who came in an elegant carriage, and who specifically asked, in the name of the President, for a thirty-hour armistice. Scott, pleased, withheld his summons and sat down and wrote a personal letter to Santa Anna, starting: "Too much blood has already been shed in this unnatural war . . ." This was a mistake. It made it look as though *Scott* was asking for an armistice, and Santa Anna deepened this impression by his reply, which treated the United States general like a petitioner, and which was given to the newspapers. The President-General himself had been careful not to mention either "peace" or "armistice," and if Mora had done so Santa Anna would unblushingly have disavowed him. Santa Anna, at the nadir of his unpopularity just then—there were rumors that he had sold out to the *norteamericanos*—could not afford to look as though *he* was suing for peace. Also, the movement gained him a little time, and time was what he desperately needed.

Accordingly, three Mexican generals met with three United States generals the night of August 22, two days after the battle, in Mackintosh's house in Tacubaya. They talked all night, and they came up with an agreement to establish an armistice of indefinite length that could be terminated by either party on a forty-eight-hour notice. This armistice should be in force everywhere within ninety miles of the capital. Neither side should be reinforced or should enlarge or strengthen its fortifications. No hostages were provided for. At one point the United States generals did venture to propose that the viceregal palace of Chapultepec, a very strong position on a rocky hill near Mexico City, should be turned over to the invaders at least for the duration of the talks. The Mexican generals recoiled in horror. Chapultepec *was* Mexico, they asserted. If the populace were to see the Stars and Stripes floating from the top of that beloved building their pride would be so stung that they would infallibly riot, undoing all of the work of the negotiators. The *norteamericanos* gave in on this point.

It is notable that the word "peace," a word of which the Mexicans seemed almost superstitiously afraid, did not occur anywhere in the agreement.

This agreement, with minor modifications, was assented to the following day by each of the commanding officers, and they promptly began to appoint commissioners, three each. Trist was to preside.

The armistice went into effect August 24.

These commissioners were good men, earnest men, and there is no doubt that all of them sincerely wanted to stop the war. There was some slight delay in their assemblage, due to the difficulty of picking Mexicans who would dare to serve. Santa Anna personally asked an ex-President, José Joaquín Herrera, to act as the chief of the Mexican delegation, and Herrera pointed out that he had been ousted from the Presidency precisely because he had favored treating with the United States before a formal state of war existed. That was exactly why they wanted and needed him now, said Santa Anna; and Herrera, a deeply patriotic fellow, acceded.

The commission met for the first time September 1, and a little earlier, only a few hours before, there had been an unfortunate incident in the city. By the terms of the armistice the United States Army could purchase supplies in the capital, and that morning a train of empty wagons went in through one of the gates for that purpose, the visit having been prearranged. The wagons were driven by civilian teamsters who were not armed; nor did any armed guard accompany them. Nevertheless, they were soon followed by a growing mob, and stones were thrown. "Yanqui, go home!" the townspeople yelled. In the central plaza, before the National Palace, the train was halted by sheer force of numbers. A company of lancers was posted nearby, but it did nothing until at last, several having been hurt, a teamster was killed. Then the lancers, somewhat languidly, dispersed the crowd, and the wagon train withdrew—without the provisions it had come to get. Obviously this demonstration had been spontaneous, not an arranged affair. Thereafter the army would send in its wagon trains at night. The city authorities apologized, and the United States Army accepted the apology; but it had been a poor way to launch peace proceedings.

The first instructions given the Mexican commissioners were manifestly framed for public consumption, not for practical work. They would have tied the commissioners' hands, making them mere recorders, clerks, giving them no power to treat, only authority to pass on to the government the ideas put forward by the United States commissioners. This was in accord with the official Mexican attitude that the United States was pleading for peace, and it would have led to an unworkable arrangement. These instructions were soon changed to make them more realistic, giving the commissioners some leeway, though this fact was not made known to the touchy Mexican public; and then the commission really got down to work.

Both sides evinced a willingness to compromise. At first the Mexicans insisted upon the Neuces as the southwestern boundary of Texas, a state they had given up all hope of getting back, and after some discussion Trist agreed to make the land between the Neuces and the Rio Grande into an independent state, a buffer state. He was exceeding his instructions when he made this agreement, and he knew it. He was also exceeding his instructions when he agreed to drop the United States demand for Lower California and the southern part of Alta California, fixing the thirty-seventh parallel of latitude as a boundary. After all, who wanted the southern part of Upper California, the Los Angeles-Monterey district? That was just wasteland. It was San Francisco Bay that the Polk administration had its eye on, and the thirty-seventh parallel agreement would give it that.

The Mexican commissioners proposed that a clause be written into the peace treaty stipulating that any territory bought by or ceded to the United States should be declared forever free from slavery. Here Nicholas P. Trist balked. He knew his Washington, and he told the Mexicans flatly that the Senate would never ratify such a treaty. They shrugged and gave up.

Everything seemed to be going swimmingly when, on September 6, the Mexican commissioners unexpectedly came to the meeting with a counterproposal, to take the place of all that had been so painfully worked out. It was ridiculous, patently made only for publication, a dictate. Among other things, it decreed that the United States indemnify Mexico for all damages done, something new in warfare, the winner paying the loser. This proposal graciously gave the United States three days in which to decide. Trist did not need that long. He closed the proceedings then and there.

In Washington the Cabinet, at a three-hour session, heard this news with indignation. It was decided to recall Trist, not only because he had exceeded his instructions but also because the presence of a member of the State Department at the front seemingly had given the proud Mexicans the thought that the United States was ready to call quits. It was decided at the same time to command Winfield Scott to resume the war in full force, not stopping until a complete surrender had been made.[44]

They might have saved themselves the trouble. The war already had been resumed.

CHAPTER

23

A Good Day's Fighting

MEXICO, D.F., was not a fortified city. No wall enclosed it. Its "gates," of which there were four facing Scott's army, were in reality only strongly built sentry houses, but each one commanded a long narrow stone causeway with marshes and ditches on either side. In other words, for military purposes the city was an island. To besiege it would require many more men, in order to encircle it, and many months of time.

An attack could be made on the city from the south or from the west. The south was watery and widespread, and its causeways were long. The west was protected by Chapultepec.

Chapultepec was a narrow volcanic ridge of rock 195 feet above ground level. It was three miles to the southwest of the central plaza of Mexico City, but it commanded the causeways that led to two gates on the west side, the San Cosme gate and the Belen gate. The ridge was 600 to 700 yards long, running almost directly east and west. The north and east sides were precipitous, the south side was steep, and the west side, the farthest from the city was rough and rocky but *could* be mounted by infantry.

Chapultepec (Hill of the Grasshoppers) was not a castle

or a fort, as so many of the northerners seemed to think. The building on it was, properly, a palace, having been constructed as a residence for the Spanish colonial viceroys. It had never been a presidential residence, and fourteen years before the invasion it had been taken over by the national military academy, thus becoming the West Point of Mexico. It was what most of the northerners meant when they spoke of the halls of Montezuma, a popular phrase of the time, though in fact the building had nothing to do with the ancient Aztec emperors.[45]

The rock, Chapultepec, was surrounded by a park of giant cypresses, all draped in Spanish moss, which in turn was surrounded by a twelve-foot stone wall—not in truth an outwork, but a piece of masonry that attackers would have to take into consideration. At the western end of this park was a group of strong stone buildings known collectively as the Molino del Rey, King's Mill. General Scott was told that this was being used as a foundry, casting cannons from melted-down church bells brought out from the city. His spies were not serving him well these days, and he did not, or could not, check this story. Less than half a mile northwest of the Molino del Rey, out in the open plain, stood a square stone building called the Casa Mata, which was known to be a powder magazine. It was believed (another mistake) that this would be easily taken.

Troops were massed and guns were emplaced on the south of the city all this while, an activity that fooled Santa Anna, who at the last moment yanked five regiments out of the Molino del Rey complex and massed them behind the southern gates.

Molino del Rey was a bloody blunder. The infantry attack was preceded by an extremely short bombardment that would seem to have done no damage at all. The buildings, especially the Casa Mata, were much stronger than had been expected, and the Mexicans who manned them fought mag-

THE BATTLE OF MOLINO DEL RAY

nificently. General William J. Worth, who was in command of the whole attack force, had previously asked permission to push on and storm Chapultepec itself from the west—if, that is, the Molino complex proved easy to take. This General Scott denied. In the middle of the struggle, Worth, a hard-bitten veteran, again asked for permission to storm the palace; and it was again denied. Certain officers, notably young Lieutenant Grant, thought that it should have been given, that the taking of the Molino buildings should have been followed up.[46]

Worth and his men had plenty of fighting as it was. They took 680 prisoners and three guns, but their own casualties came to almost 800, or about 23 percent of the whole force involved—and that in only two hours of strife.

Why? It turned out that the Molino del Rey buildings were no longer a foundry after all. No guns were made in them. The Casa Mata powder was there all right, but the invaders could not linger to haul it away, and it was blown

THE BATTLE OF CHAPULTEPEC

up. Even this action was bungled, the explosion being premature, so that twelve more men were killed.

The attackers fell back, and Santa Anna, who had been hovering nearby with reinforcements, took over the buildings, subsequently, because of this reoccupation, claiming Molino del Rey as a Mexican victory.

Chapultepec itself was a much more elaborate operation. At nine o'clock on the morning of September 12 Scott's heavy artillery opened up, and they kept firing all day and well into the night. The Mexicans replied. They had thirteen guns up there. General Nicolás Bravo had 832 regulars under him, but he also had various detached artillery units, a large body of horses (which, however, did nothing but watch), and the cadets. The cadets were no mean force in themselves. They were mere boys,[47] thirteen, fourteen, fifteen years old—those sixteen or older were already serving in the regular army—but they could handle muskets and they stood their ground. Bravo asked for reinforcements, but Santa Anna denied this request, though he promised to push in if needed. Santa Anna still thought that the real attack was about to come from the south.

Scott thought briefly of a night attack, lest the damage done by the guns be repaired during the dark hours, but he decided against this. At a little after five in the morning, which was dawn, the guns opened up again. They kept at it with everything they had until eight o'clock, when they stopped abruptly. That was the signal for the infantry advance.

They were in three columns.

Worth's took the extreme west and edged around to the northern side of the palace, where they tangled with a Mexican column sent from the city to reinforce the garrison, having a brisk little battle of their own.

Pillow had the southwest. His men, after they had beaten back the soldiers from the wall that hemmed the park, had to assault a stout circular redoubt. Beyond the re-

THE BATTLE OF MEXICO CITY

doubt were sundry upswellings of the brown earth that from a slight distance looked like freshly dug graves. But Pillow's men knew what they were: they were land mines. After that if they got past the minefield—it would be a matter of scaling ladders. There was no gate for them to smash on that side.

The gate, the only one, was on the south side, and was approached by a narrow, steep road that broke into a sharp zag about halfway up, where the fieldpiece had been placed. The men in this division had to run up that road in a shower of bullets and balls from above, for there was no cover of any sort. These men were commanded by a former professor of English literature, General J. A. Quitman, a tall, slender man with bristling gray hair, who smoked a cigar all through the fight.

The job took a little less than an hour. Pillow's men overran the redoubt with such speed that the officer in charge, a young lieutenant whose orders were to make only a token resistance and to set off the mine trains just before his retreat, hesitated to obey the second part of this command for fear he would kill many of his own men; and by the time that he had extricated himself and his following the invaders had sought out the powder trains and scattered them, so that the mines never did go off.

Then they were at the base of a steep concrete retaining wall, in effect a cliff, parapeted at the top. And there were no scaling ladders; somebody had misplaced them. They were soon found, however, and the men swarmed up like ants.

Meanwhile, Quitman's men were struggling up the road. Against the bottom of the wall of the palace at last, they were for a moment safe from fire, and they tackled that wall with crowbars. They were the second ones to reach the main court of the palace, but a close second.

There was not much fighting. It was over, there, in a few minutes; and the Mexican flag was cut down, the Stars and Stripes run up.

General Scott had given no orders as to what should be done once the palace was taken, and Worth and Quitman, whose men were in fine fettle, saw no reason to pause and pant. They plunged on.

Worth marched his men out on the Verónica causeway to the San Cosme gate, a distance of about two miles, during which they encountered only trifling opposition. After they had made a sharp turn to the right, entering the San Cosme causeway itself, the going got a great deal more tough. In the middle of the causeway there ran an aqueduct, the city's water supply, supported by small oval stone arches. These arches were large enough to protect a few crouching foot soldiers, but they would not protect the guns, and they were at best only temporary refuges. When at last the men reached a strip of the causeway that was lined with houses on both sides, they reverted to the tactics of Monterey: they smashed into the nearest house, knocked down a wall to the

GENERAL WINFIELD SCOTT ENTERING MEXICO CITY

next one, and so on, laboriously working their way to the city itself, which they reached at about six o'clock that afternoon.

Quitman took a shorter but not easier course, the Belen causeway, slightly to the south of the San Cosme causeway and very similar, supporting its own aqueduct. After an agonizing advance his men rushed and took the Belen gate at the very edge of the city, but there they were pinned down by terrific fire from the city—from rooftops, most of it.

It would soon be dark. All of the men were exhausted. Losses, as predicted, had been heavy. They were running short of ammunition, and they could not expect any reinforcement for the present. In the morning, whether or not they got any sleep, they would face the prospect of storming a city filled with street fighters in addition to Santa Anna's regulars, superior in numbers to themselves.

Then there was a great shouting at the Belen gate, and somebody was waving a white tablecloth. Warily, watchfully, fearing a trick, General Quitman (he was still smoking a cigar but he had lost one of his shoes, never finding out where or how) mounted the parapet. Santa Anna, he was told, had gathered together all that was left of his army, perhaps five thousand—desertions had been heavier than usual lately—and marched to the town of Guadalupe Hidalgo to the north.

The city was theirs.

CHAPTER

24

Fury Among the Generals

THAT ENDED THE WAR, for all practical purposes.

Santa Anna, discredited, desperate for a victory, did besiege Puebla, where Colonel Thomas Childs had about 400 able-bodied troopers and at least 1,500 sick, but the siege did not last long. September 16, Mexican Independence Day, Childs was called upon to surrender, a call that was promptly and politely refused. There was no assault, only some inconsequential skirmishing. At last the siege was lifted, and Santa Anna, who had already resigned the Presidency, was forced to resign as well his command of the army. Thereafter, as far as the War with Mexico is concerned, he fades into nothingness.[48]

More serious, not technically a part of the war but brought about because of war conditions, were the attacks upon United States Army supply trains between Vera Cruz and the capital and especially between Vera Cruz and Jalapa. These were bandit operations, prompted by hope of loot and not by military considerations.

The truth is, after the capital fell there was no longer any real national government in Mexico. The organization had simply fallen apart, and the *norteamericanos*, though aching to get home, were obliged to stay on.

Nicholas P. Trist and his firm friend General Scott were receptive, but you cannot negotiate a treaty of peace with a nongovernment.

Somehow a temporary President emerged, Manuel de la Peña y Peña, a good man, a real patriot, and soon afterward he was elected full-time President. The disappearance of Santa Anna helped. Mexican peace commissioners were appointed.

Just then Trist was curtly ordered home. He thought it over, and decided to disobey, to stay on and make the best peace treaty he could, hoping that the United States Senate would ratify it anyway. Otherwise, he feared, there would be no treaty at all, and Mexico would lapse into anarchy. He could have been right.

An armistice was in effect, and all *official* hostilities had' ceased. There were incidents in the capital, of course; there were bound to be; but on the whole the invaders behaved well, and they even came to be popular, except at the bull fights, where they insisted upon cheering for the bull.

More serious was the infighting among the generals, where charges and countercharges were hurled back and forth like grenades, and courts of inquiry and court-martial loomed. These were mostly concerned with who was to blame for what and who should get what credit, with Scott, Pillow, Worth, and Duncan the principal scrappers. The former English teacher, Quitman (he never did find that shoe), military governor of Mexico City, was not involved. These squabbles eventually were moved to Washington, all participants being summoned there. They ended in a red glow of hard feeling and name calling, having accomplished nothing except to make the army, which had just finished a superb job, look silly.

Zachary Taylor beat out Winfield Scott for the Whig nomination in 1848, and went on to be elected President.

Trist, working hard and long, if illegally, at last came

States and the citizens thereof.

In witness whereof I have hereunto set my hand, and caused the seal of the United States to be affixed

Done at the City of Washington this fourth day of July, one thousand eight hundred and forty-eight ...ndence of ...United States the seventy-third.

James K. Polk

By the President.
James Buchanan
Secretary of State.

PORTION OF THE TREATY OF GUADALUPE HIDALGO

up with a treaty that ceded to the United States, in the form of reparations, all of New Mexico and all of Upper California.

When this came before the United States Senate, which scolded Trist but took up his treaty just the same, Senator Baldwin of Connecticut offered a motion to amend it to read that no slavery should be allowed in any of the new territories ever. This was defeated twenty-eight to fifteen. The treaty itself was ratified March 10, 1848, thirty-eight to fourteen, the vote being regional rather than partisan: twenty-six Democrats and twelve Whigs for, seven of each against.

The Mexican Congress, having accepted sundry minor United States Senate modifications, ratified the treaty May 25, and five days later, at Guadalupe Hidalgo, after another burst of formalities, it went into effect. It is still in effect.

That oracle, Daniel Webster, once thundered in the Senate that California was not worth "a single dollar." In the same month in which were started the negotiations that ended with the Treaty of Guadalupe Hidalgo gold was discovered at Sutter's Mill.

Notes

1. Twenty-seven of them actually did escape. They reached the creek and after incredible hardships, and days of starvation and of wandering, they got back to safety. The exact death total will never be known, but it was probably a little over 320.

2. "But in reality he was a charlatan. Though head of an army, he knew nothing of military science; though head of a nation, he knew nothing of statesmanship. By right of superiority and by right of conquest Mexico seemed to be his; and with what Burke described as 'The generous capacity of the princely eagle,' he proposed to take the chief share of wealth, power, honor and pleasure, leaving to others the remnants of these as a compensation for doing the work." Justin Smith, *War with Mexico*, I, 54.

3. *Life in Mexico*, 65. Ruxton, that indefatigable traveler, viewed him in a somewhat different light: "His countenance completely betrays his character; indeed, I never saw a physiognomy in which the evil passions, which he notoriously possesses, were more strongly marked. Oily duplicity, treachery, avarice, and sensuality are depicted in every feature, and his well-known character bears out the truth of the impress his vices have stamped upon his face. In person he is portly, and not devoid of a certain well-bred bearing which wins him golden opinions from the surface-seeing fair sex, to whom he ever pays the most courtly attention." *Adventures in Mexico*, 30. It is only fair to add that Fanny Calderón saw him at his best, at home, whereas Ruxton met him at a low point in his up-and-down career, when his thoughts could be believed to be bitter ones.

4. "The revolt of Texas, then, was not so much revolution as resistance to revolution." Smith, *Annexation*, 13.

5. Or San Antonio de Béjar, in the Mexican fashion. It was generally called, then, either Béxar or Béjar, both of which are pronounced the same, and the San Antonio was omitted. Today it is simply San Antonio.

6. The first name of the mission had been San Antonio de Valero. Most of the members of the company garrisoned there the longest came from Alamo, a town in Coahuila, which accounts for the modern name, a nickname really, a localism, not official; or this may have been applied because of the fact that there had once been many *alamos*, or poplar trees, in that vicinity. See articles in the *Texas Historical Quarterly*, III, 67, 245.

7. So they were, in the early days of the siege. The Texan declaration of independence was not adopted until March 2 of that same year, but though this happened only a few miles away the men in the Alamo never heard of it.

8. The original of this message reposes in the Texas State Library at Austin.

9. He was in fact recalled, and it was only after long and expensive litigation that he won an acquittal. He was a capable officer, and if he had decided the other way it would have made a big difference in history.

10. Shurleff, *The Log Cabin Myth*. The symbol was to be confirmed, of course, in the campaigns of Abraham Lincoln, who actually *was* born in a log cabin.

11. He still holds these records. General Eisenhower was only sixty-six when he was elected to his second term, though before he finished that term, in 1961, he was, at seventy, the oldest man who had ever served in the White House.

12. "It seems to be one of the weaknesses of great men, in the competition for the highest honors, to prefer comparatively small men to one another." Schurz, *Henry Clay*, II, 174.

13. It could be that the name of this comparatively

humble home, and the village in which it was situated, gave the world its most widespread Americanism, the ubiquitous, mysterious, unquenchable *O.K.* Scores of explanations, many of them silly, have been looped over it. Some say that Andrew Jackson, about whom such stories habitually were told by his enemies, used to write "Oll Korrect" at the bottom of state papers of which he approved. There was supposed to have been an Obediah Kelly, or in some versions Michael O'Kelly, or Patrick O'Kelly, who was a freight agent or else a train dispatcher in Cincinnati, or maybe it was Buffalo, who used to scribble or chalk his initials on something that was ready to go. "Omnis Korrecta" was a Latin phrase old-time schoolmasters sometimes marked on test papers. Rum that came from Aux Cayes, Haiti, at one time was supposed to be the very best, the real thing, the McCoy. There was an Indian chief called Keokuk (Keokuk, Iowa, is named after him) who was wise and well liked. He was always called *Old* Keokuk, to which often was added "He's all right." The late Woodrow Wilson favored the theory that O.K. is from a Choctaw word *okeh,* meaning "it is so," and he wrote it that way, helping to popularize it. The most favored theory right now, and seemingly the best backed, is that the letters stood for Old Kinderhook—a name often linked with that of Van Buren, who was called the Sage of Kinderhook, the Magician of Kinderhook, the Fox of Kinderhook, and others. There are fliers at an earlier origin, but no satisfactory ones, and 1840 is the generally accepted date when "O.K." was first recorded as a word meaning "all right" or "satisfactory." At that time Martin Van Buren was running the Democratic machine in New York State in accordance with the boss system already established there. Anything of importance that the boys in the city wanted to do would have to be passed by him first. That is, it would have to be Old Kinderhooked, or O.K.'d. One of the toughest of the district political organizations was that of the

Democratic O.K. Club, originally located at 245 Grand Street, and when its members met other like-minded thugs —for in the New York City of that day, the day of Bill Poole and Isaiah Rynders and John Morrissey, the brickbat and the brass knuckles often scored more tellingly than the ballot—the watchword, the battlecry or slogan, frequently was "O.K." Probably we will never know the whole truth. New guesses keep popping up.

14. "Mr. Calhoun, the cast-iron man, looks as if he had never been born and could not be extinguished." Harriet Martineau, *A Retrospect of Western Travel*, XII.

15. "Neither at college nor at a later time did Polk deceive himself or attempt to deceive others by assuming great native brilliance. He never posed as one whose genius made it easy for him to decide great questions offhand. He never attempted to conceal the fact that his conclusions were reached as the result of unremitting labor." McCormac, *James K. Polk,* 4.

16. That expression in itself was to be heard only around race tracks at the time. It did not come into the political vocabulary until 1876, with the nomination and election of Rutherford Burchard Hayes, and it has been attributed to Hamilton Fish. Polk could be compared with Hayes in another respect: each was a believer in only one term for a President, and each refused even to consider running for re-election. The phrase "smoke-filled hotel-room" was not known among politicians in 1844, though the chamber itself was. "Smoke-filled hotel-room" was first used in a preconvention statement of 1920 by Harry Daugherty, Warren G. Harding's manager.

17. By way of reward Bancroft was to have been made attorney general—until the President-elect learned to his own astonishment that the man was no lawyer. Bancroft, then, was given the Navy instead.

18. It should be noted that what was called the Oregon

Territory then was a much wider spread of land than that of the present state of Oregon. It included, roughly, today's Oregon, Washington, Idaho, Montana, and British Columbia.

19. Colonel Butler was a land speculator on the side, and his presence in Mexico City was in part accounted for by that fact. Andrew Jackson, who got him the job, later repudiated the man, calling him nasty names. "It is safe to say that Butler's mission, discreditable and even disgraceful, had much to do with the unsatisfactory course of our diplomatic relations with Mexico which ended in war." Reeves, *American Diplomacy*, 68.

20. *Diary*, I, 91–93, 97, 100, 101.

21. *Diary*, I, 35.

22. A dissenting opinion: "Taylor's advance to the Bold River no more produced the war than Pitcairn's march to Lexington produced the American revolution. It was an effect and an occasion, but not a cause." Smith, *War with Mexico*, I, 154–55.

23. Boynton, *History of West Point*, 238–43.

24. "Seldom in history have two nations gone to war with such cavalier disregard for realities as did the United States and Mexico in 1846. Indifferent to the staggering problems that faced them, innocent of having conceived even the most elementary plan of campaign, wholly unprepared, each country entered the conflict with an enormously exaggerated view of its own strength and with a feeling of contempt for the other." Singletary, *The Mexican War*, 20.

25. This was the same Braxton Bragg who in a later war was to be such a controversial figure as a Confederate general.

26. It is, of course, today Brownsville.

27. To a European or anyone tutored in conventional warfare the idea of dragoons attacking on horseback is absurd. Properly, and originally, the dragoon was not a

cavalryman but an infantryman, trained and officered as such. He fought on foot, and used his horse only as a means of transportation. This distinction, however, was breaking down; and in America it had never been respected. "Dragoon" in America was simply a fancy name for a horse soldier. The dragoons who covered themselves with glory at Resaca de la Palma carried sabers as well as carbines and were trained to fight in saddle.

28. "All the drinking-water to be had was from the river, a tepid mixture about thirty per cent. sand and the rest half yellow mud. Against the purgative effect of a full draught there was nothing available except a pill of opium." Wallace, *Autobiography*, I, 123–24. This self-assured young man, Lewis Wallace, was to rise in the Civil War to the rank of major general, and afterward to become governor of the Territory of New Mexico and minister to Turkey. It was in New Mexico that he finished his second novel, a tale laid in Rome at the time of Jesus. It was a bulky, bulgy thing, and the publishers, Harper & Brothers, were leery of it, for historicals were not selling well at just that time. His first novel, *The Fair God*, had done all right, however, and it was for this reason that they published the second, attaching to it the forbidding price tag of $1.50, late in 1880. It got off to a slow start, but the second year (most novels do not sell that long) it picked up a bit, and the third year it really shot ahead. A long-run play was made from it, and two expensive movies. The book itself sold 2,600,000 copies in the United States alone. Its title? *Ben-Hur*. Frank Luther Mott, *Golden Multitudes* (New York: The Macmillan Company, 1947), 172–74.

29. "The place is quite Americanized by our army and the usual train of sutlers, etc., etc.—you can get anything you want there." McClellan, *Mexican Diary*, 12. This young letter writer, a lieutenant then, was destined to lead the Army of the Potomac in the Civil War.

30. "No European pretender—Stuart, Bourbon, or any other—ever offered to sell out his country with a more barefaced cynicism. No unscrupulous foreign government ever fell into a pretender's trap more easily." Stephenson, *Texas and the Mexican War*, 191.

31. He was best known to the public as the young officer who had arrested Aaron Burr when that adventurer was fleeing in disguise after the collapse of his Mississippi-Mexico expedition. Gainesville, Florida, the seat of the state university, and also Gainesville, Texas, were named after him.

32. La Angostura is the Mexican name for the battle that was to follow, though the *norteamericanos* called it Buena Vista from the large hacienda of that name a few miles to the north. The Mexican name is perhaps more accurate, for much of the fighting took place in or near the Narrows, very little in the hacienda.

33. In fact, O'Brien was a captain at this time, though he did not know it. His promotion was on its way to the front. Thomas, of course, was to become the famous "Rock of Chickamauga."

34. President Polk, worried about these allegations and the effect that they might have on the prolongation of the war, had summoned to the White House the Roman Catholic bishops of St. Louis and New York, and had asked them if they could assign some Spanish-speaking priests as chaplains to the army. *Diary*, I, 408–11. Chaplains in those days could not, by law, be commissioned into the army. They served as civilian employees. Rives, *United States*, II, 227–28.

35. "The country was a succession of cups of sand; the only redeeming thing about this part of the march, was that we heard the sweet, sometimes plaintive, sometimes cheerful notes of the birds in the recesses of the glades." Anderson, *Artillery Officer*, 133. This letter writer, a good one, was

a captain at the time. Later, as a major, he was to be the commanding officer at Fort Sumter when it was attacked in the opening fight of the War Between the States. His second-in-command at that latter post was to be Abner Doubleday, the man who invented baseball.

A story has it that the word "gringo" originated here, when the Yanqui troops marched out of Vera Cruz, the peasants picking it up from the first line of a Robert Burns ballad the soldiers used to sing:

> Green grow the rashes O,
> Green grow the rashes O;
> The sweetest hours that e'er I spend,
> Are spent among the lasses O!

However, the late Dr. Frank H. Vizetelly traced it back to a dictionary published in Spain in 1787, which defines a gringo as a foreigner, especially an Irishman, who has trouble with his Spanish. Henry L. Mencken, *American Language* (New York: Alfred A. Knopf), Supplement I, 638–39.

36. The reader might be reminded that the word "telegraph" is very old, being from the Greek "afar-writer," and does not always apply, as it does today, merely to the invention of Samuel F. B. Morse. An Indian smoke signal, for instance, could properly be called a telegraph; and so could a semaphore, or a flashed code. The Morse invention, for many years after its first appearance, was called an *electric* telegraph.

37. *Memoirs*, I, 132–33.

38. According to rumors, none of them verifiable, the loot also included Santa Anna's wooden leg. At any rate, an inestimable number of these articles were sold after the battle as souvenirs.

39. Polk, *Diary*, III, 58.

40. Later, as Sir Edward Thornton, he was to serve for many years as British ambassador at Washington.

41. Scott, *Memoirs*, II, 466.

42. "Oh, Veracruz! Such environs! The surrounding houses black with smoke of powder or with fire—the streets deserted—a view of melancholy bare red sandhills all around—not a tree, or shrub, or flower, or bird, except the horrid black zopilote, or police officer. All looks as though the prophet Jeremiah had passed through the city denouncing woe to all the dwellers thereof. It is enough to make one feel homesick. Such a melancholy, wholly deserted-looking burial ground as we saw!" Calderón, *Life in Mexico*, 59.

43. "The *Fortaleza*, or Castle as it is called, is situated on a plain, about half a mile from town. The main work is a tower, surrounded by a large square, the angles of which are bastioned, the whole having a ditch around it. The walls of the inner work which formed the exterior walls of the quarters are three feet thick. This place has been at various times the prison of some of Mexico's greatest men." Anderson, *Artillery Officer*, 143.

44. "The unofficial information received shows that Mexico has refused to treat for peace upon terms which the U.S. can accept; and it is now manifest that the war must be prosecuted with increased forces and increased energy. We must levy contributions and quarter on the enemy. This is part of the object of the letter to Gen'l Scott. Mr. Trist is recalled because his remaining longer with the army could not, probably, accomplish the objects of his mission, and because his remaining longer might, & probably would, impress the Mexican Government with the belief that the U.S. were so anxious for peace that they would ultimately conclude one upon the Mexican terms. Mexico must now first sue for peace, & when she does we will hear her propositions.

"The Cabinet remained upwards of three hours, and

when they adjourned I found myself much exhausted & fatigued." Polk, *Diary*, III, 186.

45. There was a battalion of three hundred Marines in Scott's army, and this gave the author of the U.S. Marines' song (himself unknown, though the music of course is Offenbach's) the right to write:

From the halls of Montezuma
To the shores of Trip-o-li—

He meant Chapultepec.

46. Grant, *Memoirs*, I, 152.

47. In Mexican histories they are known, affectionately, as Los Niños, or the Little Boys. Several were killed. They wore bright blue hats with tassels, very brave. There is a statue of them in the present-day Chapultepec, a national shrine.

48. But not as far as the history of Mexico itself is concerned. Disgraced, he was exiled in 1848, just before the war was formally terminated, this time to Jamaica; but he was soon back and made President for life, with the title Supreme Highness. That was in 1853, and he lasted about two years, after which he made a hasty trip to Europe. He spent the rest of his life—he died June 20, 1876, age eighty-one—trying to get back into the Presidential palace. He intrigued with France, with the United States, with the Emperor Maximilian, who gave him the empty title of grand marshal but nothing more. In 1867 he was arrested while trying to stir up a revolution, and was condemned to death but pardoned because he was so clearly in his dotage. That was the end of Antonio Lopez de Santa Anna. See Hanighen, Callcott, and Bancroft, in the *Bibliography*.

A Note on the Sources

BECAUSE IT WAS so soon overshadowed by the War Between the States, and also because many Americans think of the Mexican War with embarrassment, and even a touch of shame, the belief seems widespread that not much has been written about it. The contrary is true. They were a highly articulate lot, those boys who marched off to Texas and to Mexico, and today's shelves are packed with their letters and diaries, their journals and reminiscences. The on-the-spot descriptions were preferred to those written many years later in the form of ponderous memoirs, but both have been useful.

In addition, this period and its personalities of late have caught the fancy of many a cloistered scholar, as evidenced by the large percentage of university press imprints among the books listed below, a list selective but by no means exhaustive.

My thanks are due to the reference librarians at the Olin Library, Wesleyan University; the Palmer Library, Connecticut College for Women; the Phoebe Griffin Noyes Library, Old Lyme, Connecticut, and the Yale University Library.

Bibliography

ADAMS, EPHRAIM. *British Interests and Activities in Texas, 1838-1846.* Baltimore: The Johns Hopkins Press, 1910.

ANDERSON, ROBERT. *An Artillery Officer in the Mexican War, 1846-7.* New York and London: G. P. Putnam's Sons, 1911.

BANCROFT, HUBERT HOWE. *History of the North Mexican States and Texas.* Vols. I and II. San Francisco: A. L. Bancroft & Company, 1889.

BARKER, EUGENE C. *The Life of Stephen F. Austin, Founder of Texas, 1793-1836.* Nashville and Dallas: The Cokesbury Press, 1926.

———. *Mexico and Texas, 1821-1835.* New York: Russell & Russell, Inc., 1965

———. "President Jackson and the Texas Revolution." *American Historical Review*, Vol. XII, p. 788.

BEMIS, SAMUEL FLAGG. *The Latin American Policy of the United States: An Historical Interpretation.* New York: Harcourt, Brace and Company, 1943.

BENTON, THOMAS HART. *Thirty Years View; or, A History of the working of the American government for thirty years, from 1820 to 1850.* 2 vols. New York and London: D. Appleton and Company, 1854-58.

BILL, ALFRED HOYT. *Rehearsal for Conflict: The War with Mexico, 1846-1848.* New York: Alfred A. Knopf, 1947.

BINKLEY, WILLIAM C., ed. *Official Correspondence of the Texas Revolution, 1835-1836.* 2 vols. New York: D. Appleton-Century Company, 1936.

———. *The Texas Revolution.* Baton Rouge: Louisiana State University Press, 1952.

182 Bibliography

BISHOP, FARNHAM. *Our First War in Mexico.* New York: Charles Scribner's Sons, 1916.

BLACKWOOD, EMMA JEANNE, see SMITH, CAPTAIN E. KIRBY.

BOURNE, E. G. "The Proposed Absorption of Mexico in 1847–1848." *Annual Report of the American Historical Association for 1899,* Vol. I, pp. 157–69. Washington, 1900.

BOYNTON, CAPTAIN EDWARD CARLISLE. *History of West Point, and the Origin and Progress of the United States Military Academy.* New York: D. Van Nostrand, 1863.

BRADY, CYRUS TOWNSEND. *The Conquest of the Southwest: The Story of a Great Spoliation.* New York: D. Appleton Company, 1905.

BROOKS, N. C. *A Complete History of the Mexican War.* Philadelphia, 1849.

BROWN, JOHN HENRY. *History of Texas, from 1685 to 1892.* 2 vols. St. Louis, 1893.

BRUCE, HAROLD R. *American Parties and Politics: History and Role of Political Parties in the United States.* New York: Henry Holt and Company, 1927.

CALDERÓN DE LA BARCA, FANNY. *Life in Mexico: The Letters of Fanny Calderón de la Barca, with New Material from the Author's Private Journals.* Edited and annotated by Howard T. Fisher and Marion Hall Fisher. Garden City: Doubleday and Company, Inc., 1966.

CALLAHAN, JAMES MORTON. *American Foreign Policy in Mexican Relations.* New York: The Macmillan Company, 1932.

CALLCOTT, WILFRED HARDY. *Santa-Anna: The Story of an Enigma Who Once Was Mexico.* Norman: University of Oklahoma Press, 1936.

CHABOT, FREDERICK C., see TRUEHEART, JAMES L.

CHANNING, EDWARD. *A History of the United States.* 6 vols. New York: The Macmillan Company, 1926.

Bibliography

DEVOTO, BERNARD. *The Year of Decision, 1846.* Boston: Houghton Mifflin Company, 1943.

DRUMM, ELLEN M. see MAGOFFIN, SUSAN SHELBY.

DYER, BRAINERD. *Zachary Taylor.* Baton Rouge: Louisiana State University Press, 1946.

ELLIOTT, CHARLES WINSLOW. *Winfield Scott, the Soldier and the Man.* New York: The Macmillan Company, 1937.

ESPOSITO, COLONEL VINCENT J., ed. *The West Point Atlas of American Wars.* New York: Frederick A. Praeger, 1959.

FISH, CARL RUSSELL. *The Rise of the Common Man, 1830–1850.* New York: The Macmillan Company, 1927.

FISHER, HOWARD T., see CALDERÓN DE LA BARCA, FANNY.

FISHER, MARION HALL, see CALDERÓN DE LA BARCA, FANNY.

FOOTE, HENRY STUART. *Texas and the Texans.* 2 vols. Philadelphia: Thomas, Cowperthwait & Company, 1841.

FROST, J. *The Mexican War and Its Warriors.* New Haven: H. Mansfield, 1848.

GAMBRELL, HERBERT. *Anson Jones, the Last President of Texas.* Garden City: Doubleday and Company, Inc., 1948.

GANOE, WILLIAM ADDLEMAN. *The History of the United States Army.* New York and London: D. Appleton-Century Company, 1943. (revised edition)

GARRISON, GEORGE PIERCE. "The First Stage of the Movement for the Annexation of Texas." *American Historical Review,* Vol. X, pp. 72–96.

GIDDINGS, LUTHER. *Sketches of the Campaign in Northern Mexico, in Eighteen Forty-six and Seven.* New York: G. P. Putnam & Company, 1853.

GRAEBNER, NORMAN A. *Empire on the Pacific.* New York: The Ronald Press Company, 1955.

GRANT, U. S. *Personal Memoirs of U. S. Grant.* 2 vols. New York: Charles L. Webster & Company, 1886.

GUNDERSON, ROBERT GRAY. *The Log-Cabin Campaign.* Louisville: The University of Kentucky Press, 1957.

HAMILTON, HOLMAN. *Zachary Taylor, Soldier of the Republic.* Indianapolis: The Bobbs-Merrill Company, 1941.

HANIGHEN, FRANK C. *Santa Anna, The Napoleon of the West.* New York: Coward-McCann, Inc., 1934.

HATCHER, MATTIE AUSTIN. *The Opening of Texas to Foreign Settlement, 1801-1821.* Austin: The University of Texas Press, 1927.

HENRY, ROBERT SELPH. *The Story of the Mexican War.* Indianapolis: The Bobbs-Merrill Company, 1950.

HENRY, W. S. *Campaign Sketches of the War with Mexico.* New York: Harper & Brothers, 1847.

HOFSTADTER, RICHARD. *The American Political Tradition.* New York: Alfred A. Knopf, 1954.

HOGAN, WILLIAM RANSOM. *The Texas Republic: a Social and Economic History.* Norman: The University of Oklahoma Press, 1946.

HORGAN, PAUL. *Great River: The Rio Grande in American History.* 2 vols. New York: Rinehart and Company, 1954.

HOUSTON, ANDREW JACKSON. *Texas Independence.* Houston: The Anson Jones Press, 1938.

JAMES, MARQUIS. *The Raven: A Biography of Sam Houston.* Indianapolis: The Bobbs-Merrill Company, 1929.

JAY, WILLIAM. *A Review of the Causes and Consequences of the Mexican War.* Boston: Benjamin B. Mussey & Co., 1849.

JENKINS, JOHN S. *James Knox Polk.* Auburn, N.Y.: J. M. Alden, 1851.

KEARNY, THOMAS. *General Philip Kearny, Battle Soldier in Five Wars.* New York: G. P. Putnam's Sons, 1937.

KELEHER, WILLIAM A. *A Turmoil in New Mexico, 1846-1848.* Santa Fe: The Rydal Press, 1952.

KENDALL, GEORGE WILKINS. *The War Between the United States and Mexico*. New York and Philadelphia, 1851.

KENLY, JOHN R. *Memoirs of a Maryland Volunteer of the War with Mexico, in the Years 1846-7-8*. Philadelphia: J. B. Lippincott & Co., 1873.

LADD, HORATIO O. *History of the War with Mexico*. New York: Dodd, Mead and Company, 1883.

LAVENDER, DAVID. *Climax at Buena Vista: The American Campaigns in Northeastern Mexico*. Philadelphia: J. B. Lippincott Company, 1966.

LAVENPORT, HARBERT. "The Men of Goliad." *Southwestern Historical Quarterly*, Vol. XLIII (1939), pp. 1-41.

LUNDY, BENJAMIN. *The War in Texas*. Philadelphia, 1837.

McCLELLAN, GENERAL GEORGE B. *Mexican Diary*. Edited by W. S. Myers. Princeton: Princeton University Press, 1917.

McCORMAC, EUGENE IRVING. *James K. Polk, a Political Biography*. New York: Russell & Russell, Inc., 1965.

McCOY, CHARLES A. *Polk and the Presidency*. Austin: University of Texas Press, 1960.

MAGOFFIN, SUSAN SHELBY. *Down the Santa Fe Trail and into Mexico: The Diary of Susan Shelby Magoffin, 1846-1847*. New Haven: Yale University Press, 1926.

MANSFIELD, EDWARD D. *The Life and Services of General Winfield Scott*. New York: A. S. Barnes & Company, 1852.

MARSHALL, T. M. *The Western Boundary of the Louisiana Purchase*. Berkeley: University of California Press, 1914.

MERK, FREDERICK. *The Monroe Doctrine and American Expansion, 1843-1849*. New York: Alfred A. Knopf, 1966.

MINNIGERODE, MEADE. *The Fabulous Forties, 1840-1850*. New York: G. P. Putnam's Sons, 1924.

———. *Presidential Years, 1787-1860*. New York: G. P. Putnam's Sons, 1928.

MORISON, SAMUEL ELIOT, see SHURLEFF, HAROLD R.

MYERS, WILLIAM STARR, see MCCLELLAN, GEORGE B.

NANCE, JOSEPH MILTON. *After San Jacinto: The Texas-Mexican Frontier, 1836–1841.* Austin: University of Texas Press, 1963.

———. *Attack and Counterattack: The Texas-Mexican Frontier, 1842.* Austin: University of Texas Press, 1964.

NEVINS, ALLAN, see STRONG, GEORGE TEMPLETON.

NICHOLS, ROY F. *The Stakes of Power, 1845–1877.* New York: Hill and Wang, 1961.

OWEN, CHARLES H. *The Justice of the Mexican War, a review of the causes and results of the war, with a view to distinguishing evidence from opinion and inference.* New York and London: G. P. Putnam's Sons, 1908.

PARISH, JOHN CARL. *The Emergence of the Idea of Manifest Destiny.* Los Angeles: The University of California Press, 1932.

POLK, JAMES K. *The Diary of James K. Polk, during his presidency, 1845 to 1849,* edited by Milo Milton Quaife. 4 vols. Chicago: A. C. McClurg & Company, 1910.

PRATT, JULIUS W. "The Origin of 'Manifest Destiny'." *American Historical Review,* Vol. XXXII (July, 1927).

QUAIFE, MILO MILTON, see POLK, JAMES K.

RAMSEY, ALBERT C., ed. *The Other Side; or Notes for the History of the War between Mexico and the United States,* translated from the Spanish. New York: John Wiley, 1850.

REEVES, JESSE S. *American Diplomacy under Tyler and Polk.* Baltimore: The Johns Hopkins Press, 1907.

RIPLEY, ROSWELL SABINE. *The War with Mexico.* 2 vols. New York: Harper & Brothers, 1849.

RIVES, GEORGE LOCKHART. *The United States and Mexico, 1821–1848.* 2 vols. New York: Charles Scribner's Sons, 1913.

Bibliography

ROSEBOOM, EUGENE H. *A History of Presidential Elections.* New York: The Macmillan Company, 1957.

ROYCE, JOSIAH. *California, from the Conquest in 1846 to the Second Vigilance Committee in San Francisco: A Study in American Character.* Boston: Houghton Mifflin & Company, 1886.

RUIZ, RAMON EDUARDO. *The Mexican War—was it manifest destiny?* New York: Holt, Rinehart and Winston, 1963.

RUXTON, GEORGE F. *Adventures in Mexico and the Rocky Mountains.* New York: Harper & Brothers, 1848.

SCHURZ, CARL. *Henry Clay.* 2 vols. Boston: Houghton Mifflin & Company, 1887.

SCOTT, WINFIELD. *Memoirs of Lieut.-General Scott.* 2 vols. New York: Sheldon & Company, 1864.

SELLERS, CHARLES. *James K. Polk, Continentalist, 1843–1846.* Princeton: Princeton University Press, 1966.

———. *James K. Polk, Jacksonian, 1795–1843.* Princeton: Princeton University Press, 1957.

SHEPARD, EDWARD M. *Martin Van Buren.* Boston: Houghton Mifflin & Company, 1890.

SHURLEFF, HAROLD R. *The Log Cabin Myth: A Study of the Early Dwellings of the English Colonists in North America.* Introduction by Samuel Eliot Morison. Cambridge: Harvard University Press, 1939.

SINGLETARY, OTIS A. *The Mexican War.* Chicago: The University of Chicago Press, 1960.

SMITH, ARTHUR D. HOWDEN. *Old Fuss and Feathers, Life and Exploits of Lieutenant General Winfield Scott.* New York: The Greystone Press, 1937.

SMITH, CAPTAIN E. KIRBY. *To Mexico with Scott: letters of Captain E. Kirby Smith to his wife,* edited by Emma Jeanne Blackwood. Cambridge: Harvard University Press, 1917.

SMITH, JUSTIN H. *The Annexation of Texas.* New York: Barnes and Noble, Inc., 1941.

———. *The War with Mexico.* 2 vols. New York: The Macmillan Company, 1919.

STEPHENSON, NATHANIEL W. *Texas and the Mexican War.* New Haven: Yale University Press, 1919.

STEVENS, MAJOR ISAAC INGALLS. *Campaigns of the Rio Grande and of Mexico.* New York: D. Appleton and Company, 1851.

STRONG, GEORGE TEMPLETON, *Diary.* 4 vols. Edited by Allan Nevins. New York: The Macmillan Company, 1952.

THORPE, T. B. *Our Army on the Rio Grande.* Philadelphia: Carey and Harte, 1846.

TRUEHEART, JAMES L. *The Perote Prisoners: Being the Diary of James L. Trueheart printed for the first time together with an historical introduction by Frederick C. Chabot.* San Antonio: The Nayor Company, 1934.

WALLACE, LEW. *Autobiography.* 2 vols. New York and London: Harper & Brothers, 1906.

WEBB, WALTER PRESCOTT. *The Texas Rangers; a century of frontier defense.* Boston: Houghton Mifflin Company, 1935.

WISEHART, M. K. *Sam Houston: American Giant.* Washington: Robert B. Luce, Inc., 1962.

WORLEY, J. L. "The Diplomatic Relations of England and the Republic of Texas." *Quarterly of the State Historical Association,* July, 1905.

WRIGHT, GENERAL MARCUS J. *General Scott.* New York: D. Appleton and Company, 1900.

YOAKUM, HENDERSON. *History of Texas, from its first settlement to its annexation by the United States in 1846.* 2 vols. New York: Redfield, 1850.

Index

Adams, John Quincy, 69, 78
Alamo, the, 21–30, 34, 37–8, 41, 56; Note 6
Almonte, Colonel, 34, 38, 41, 43
Ampudia, General Pedro de, 85–6, 89, 105
Arista, General Mariano, 86, 88, 91, 93–4, 97
Armijo, Governor, 96
Atocha, General A. J., 81–2
Austin, Moses, 18

Baldwin, Senator Roger S., 169
Bancroft, George, 66; Note 17
Bankhead, Charles, 143
Baudin, Admiral, 45
Benton, Thomas Hart, 120
Bernard, Dr., 11, 13
Bocanegra, Señor, 58–9
Bowie, Colonel James, 22, 24
Bragg, Lieutenant Braxton, 118; Note 25
Bravo, General Nicolas, 161
Brown, Major Jacob, 89, 90; Note 26
Buchanan, James, 64–5, 78, 82, 95, 143, 152
Buena Vista, Battle of, 114–18
Burnet, David G., 34
Burr, Aaron, 50; Note 31
Bustamante, President, 17, 44
Butler, Anthony, 75; Note 19

Cadwalader, Colonel John, 140, 144
Calderón, Fannie, 16, Note 42
Calhoun, John, 64–5, 72–3; Note 14
Carson, Kit, 96
Cass, Lewis, 64–6
Castrillon, General, 38
Cerro Gordo, Battle of, 135–39, 144, 148
Clay, Henry, 49, 50, 53, 62–3, 67, 72
Clay, Henry, Jr., 113
Conner, Commodore David, 79, 108, 121, 126
Cos, General Perfecto de, 23, 25, 27, 35, 37
Crockett, Davy, 23–5, 27, 29

Dallas, George M., 67
Davis, Jefferson, 113
Doniphan, Colonel Alexander W., 96
Doubleday, Abner, Note 35

Edson, Captain Alvin, 127
Ellis, Powhatan, 75

Fannin, Colonel James W., 9, 10, 11, 14
Farragut, Commander David, 45
Filisola, General Vincenza, 42; Note 9

Frelinghuysen, Theodore, 62
Frémont, Captain John Charles, 96

Gaines, Major General Edmund Pendleton, 107; Note 31
Goliad, massacre at, 9–14, 34, 56
Grant, Lieutenant U. S., 84, 159

Hamilton, Alexander, 50
Harney, Colonel William S., 136
Harrison, William Henry, 49, 50–3, 71; Note 11
Henry, Sergeant Thomas, 138
Herrera, President José Joaquín, 76, 78, 81, 154
Houston, Sam, 31–3, 35–8, 41–3, 45, 54, 56–7

Iturbide, Emperor Augustín de, 17

Jackson, Andrew, 43–4, 47–8, 70–1, 78
Jefferson, Joseph, 100
Jefferson, Thomas, 47
Johnson, Cave, 65
Johnson, Colonel Richard M., 48, 64–5
Jones, Commodore Thomas ap Catesby, 58–9, 60–1, 79

Kearny, Brigadier General Stephen W., 95–6, 107
Kendall, George Wilkins, 55

Lamar, Mirabeau Buonaparte, 54–5
Landero, General Juan de, 129
Larkin, Thomas O., 79
Lee, Captain Robert E., 135

Mackenzie, Commodore Alexander Slidell, 102–3
Mackintosh, Mr., 152–53
Madison, James, 47
Marcy, William Learned, 109, 142–43
Mejía, General Francisco, 85, 98–9
Micheltorena, Governor, 60–1
Mora y Villamil, General Ignacio, 152
Morales, Governor Juan, 124, 128–29

O'Brien, Lieutenant John Paul Jones, 118; Note 33
O'Donell, Don Leopoldo, 81

Pacheo, Ramón, 152
Paredes y Arrillaga, General Mariano, 76, 78, 81, 94
Parrott, W. S., 76
Patterson, Major General Robert, 134
Peña y Peña, President Manuel de la, 167
Perry, Commodore Matthew, 126
Perry, Commodore Oliver Hazard, 126
Pierce, Franklin, 146

Pillow, Colonel Gideon, 138, 161–62, 167
Poinsett, Joel Roberts, 75
Polk, James K., 66–7, 75–9, 80, 86, 96, 102, 106, 108–9, 120, 134; Note 15, Note 34
Portilla, Lieutenant Colonel, 12, 13

Quitman, General J. A., 162–63, 165, 167

Remontel, Monsieur, 44
Resaca de la Palma, action at, 91, 93–4, 97
Riley, Brigadier General Bennett, 138
Roorbach, Baron, 67
Rusk, Thomas, 36

Salezar, Captain, 56
San Jacinto, Battle of, 33–9, 68
Santa Anna, Antonio López de, 13, 15–7, 20–1; and the Alamo, 22–3, 27–8; captured, 33–5, 37–9, 40–4; marches north, 45–6, 56–7; and Cuba, 75–6, 81–2; return to Mexico, 102–3, 108–9, 110–14, 115, 117; retreats, 126, 132–34, 138–39, 143–44, 147, 149; treats for peace, 150–54; fall of, 161, 166–67; Notes 2 and 3, Note 48
Scott, Winfield, 49; takes command, 107–9, 110–11, 113–14; before Vera Cruz, 119, 120–22, 127–28; toward Mexico City, 133, 138–39, 140, 142–44, 146; peace moves, 150–53, 156; storming of Mexico City, 158, 161, 163; peace, 167
Shackleford, Doctor, 11, 13
Shannon, Wilson, 75
Slidell, John, 75, 77–8
Sloat, Commodore John D., 79
Smith, Erastus ("Deaf"), 36
Smith, Brigadier General Persifor, 143
Somerville, General, 57–8
Stewart, Commodore Charles, 64–5
Stockton, Commodore Robert F., 96

Tatnall, Commander Josiah, 122
Taylor, Zachary, 80, 82–4, 86, 88–9, 90–1, 93–4, 96–9, 101, 104–6, 108–9, 111–13, 117, 141, 167
Thomas, Lieutenant George H., 118; Note 33
Thompson, Waddy, 75
Thornton, Edward, 143, 152; Note 40
Thornton, Captain Seth, 86
Travis, Lieutenant Colonel William Barret, 22, 24–6
Trist, Nicholas P., 141–44, 146, 155–56, 167, 169; Note 44
Twiggs, Brigadier General David E., 134
Tyler, John, 50, 53, 63, 71–5

Upshur, Abel P., 72
Urrea, General, 10, 11

Van Buren, Martin, 47–8, 52–3, 63, 65–7, 70–2
Vanderlinden, Doctor, 115
Vásquez, General Rafael, 57

Ward, Lieutenant Colonel, 14
Washington, George, 47
Washington, Captain John M., 117

Webster, Daniel, 49, 62, 71, 169
Woll, Colonel Adrian, 57
Woodbury, Senator Levi, 65
Wool, Brigadier General John E., 105–6, 110, 114, 117
Worth, Brigadier General William Jenkins, 104, 130, 159, 163, 167
Wright, Hendrick B., 65
Wright, Silas, 66–67

Yell, Colonel Archibald, 113